By Christopher Catherwood

THE EVERYTHING YOU NEED TO KNOW SERIES

The Battles of World War I
The Battles of World War II
One Hundred Years of Protest

a&b

ONE HUNDRED YEARS OF PROTEST:

Everything You Need to Know

CHRISTOPHER CATHERWOOD

Allison & Busby Limited
12 Fitzroy Mews
London W1T 6DW
allisonandbusby.com

First published in Great Britain by Allison & Busby in 2015.

A CIP catalogue record for this book is available from
the British Library.

First Edition

ISBN 978-0-7490-1517-6

Typeset in 10.75/15.75 pt Adobe Garamond Pro by
Allison & Busby Ltd.

The paper used for this Allison & Busby publication
has been produced from trees that have been legally sourced
from well-managed and credibly certified forests.

Printed and bound by
CPI Group (UK) Ltd, Croydon, CR0 4YY

To the loving memory of my father
Frederick Catherwood
1925–2014

And to his daughter-in-law, my wife
Paulette

TABLE OF CONTENTS

INTRODUCTION

What do we want? A Student Union!
When do we want it? Now!
What are we wearing? Dirty jerseys!

The chants of hundreds of thousands of students down the ages are very similar to the first four lines of the above extract. The final lines are rather unusual, however, and possibly unique. It never occurred to people in Oxford back in the autumn of 1973 that *Oxford* university students would ever demonstrate or chant about anything. Yes, students in Paris might riot (as they did so spectacularly in 1968), but in Britain – and at *Oxford*? The thought was inconceivable to many observers, who could not quite believe their eyes when they saw large numbers of Oxford students with placards walking down the High Street and 'the Broad', all vociferously demanding the same kind of university-wide student union as existed at virtually every other British university – except, of course, at Cambridge . . .

They could not be Oxford students, opined the great Lady Alexandra Trevor-Roper, wife of Regius Professor Hugh Trevor-Roper and herself the daughter of Field Marshal the Earl Haig, commander of British forces in the First World War. And how did she know this? The demonstrators were wearing dirty jerseys! They could not possibly be Oxford!

So from then on it became de rigeur among certain of the Oxford university student political classes not merely to shave the night before (so as to have a day's growth of beard, as intellectuals seemed to have in France), or to have hair slightly *below* the collar, but also to wear a *dirty* jersey. This was done not out of absent-mindedness, though there was plenty of that as always among students, but as a mark of honour, a dirty-jersey-wearing *Oxford* student.

The student union never came. The monopoly enjoyed by college bars continues – and probably does so to this day. Several very talented students were 'sent down' or expelled, one of whom is now a nationally revered journalist who went on to great things after leaving Oxford. Those of us of a more nervous disposition visited the illegally occupied building chosen by the protesters just once, always slightly apprehensive that the authorities would strike while *we* were in the building. Some of us actually remembered that we were at university to work, knuckled down to some serious study, and passed our prelim exams.

The building occupied by dozens of eager protesters is now a Faculty library, filled with students far more anxious to get a good degree and a well-paid job on graduation than to waste time protesting about things that can never happen.

But in 1973 the whiff of revolution still hovered over Balliol

College Oxford, with the presence of 'The Hitch', otherwise known as the writer Christopher Hitchens, still there in spirit though no longer in person. Balliol students were so outraged at the military coup in Chile in 1973 that they unanimously passed a resolution asking General Pinochet to step down to let the revolution continue. The mind boggled – did a military dictator really cower in fright when a bunch of Oxford students asked him to resign? *Pinochet Terrified by Oxford Student Demand – Flees the Country!* None of us ever read *that* headline over our baked beans for breakfast. Yet absurd and ludicrous though it all now looks over forty years later, they were in one sense exciting times. People in those days actually *believed* in something, they *cared* . . . How true is that today? Has a strong dose of realism – often caused by the spectre of unemployment in these financially uncertain times – brought with it a sense of selfishness, of being out just for oneself and one's own future, of lack of concern for other people and especially those less fortunate than oneself? One wonders . . .

Perspective brings a degree of wisdom and now we live in an age where the terrors are very different from those of my student days. We no longer fear nuclear war, the threat of Armageddon with Soviet missiles obliterating one half of the earth and American missiles the other. But we have terrorism, which brings its own fears, and possibly another kind of annihilation, *if* the environmental activists are right about the dangers of global warming. There are still many issues about which to protest and against which to demonstrate, even if the targets have changed since the student demonstrations of a long time ago.

This book is about the past century or so of protest movements.

It would have been possible to take it further back, to look at the Peasant's Revolt of the fourteenth century, the Boston Tea Party and the French Revolution, the heroic movements to free the slaves in Britain and the USA, and many more besides. Unfortunately the book would then have been impossibly long, so the publishers wisely decided to start the clock at 1900 and take it from there.

Even so, many protests have to be omitted. And many of them were small but highly significant. For example, the women portrayed in the film *Made in Dagenham* may not be world famous, but they struck a solid blow for equal pay for female as well as male workers that has proved significant. Local protests might not achieve much in and of themselves, but *cumulatively* they can create a momentum that truly changes the world. Communism in Romania seemed immoveable in 1989, and many reckoned that while other Soviet-bloc regimes would fall, in Bucharest it would remain. But demonstrations against the mistreatment of a single individual in a provincial town eventually set a light that in the end caused the overthrow of even the Ceauşescu regime, an event that the wisest commentators thought impossible. And the whole Arab Spring, as we shall see, began when an obscure street vendor in Tunisia committed suicide.

So this book is inevitably a selection of protest movements, rather than being a much longer definitive account. Unfortunately, so much written about what are called 'social movements' by the academics are in impenetrable sociological prose, readable only by those who have spent time at university learning to master the jargon and arcane terminology. Online media sources can be very helpful, but can also often be put together by enthusiasts, and so are not always as objective as one would wish.

Perspective is also always vital in looking at protest movements. That is why our book looks at two protest movements in two countries that in the short term looked like failures but in the long term were successes: Czechoslovakia in 1968 and then in 1989, and Poland in both 1980 and also in 1989. The Prague Spring of 1968 was crushed with Soviet tanks and over twenty years of brutal Communist oppression. But then in 1989 came the Velvet Revolution and the astonishingly bloodless overthrow of the hitherto seemingly invincible Communist Party. It was similar in Poland. In 1980 Solidarity, the free Trade Union, flourished briefly, only in its turn to be suppressed, this time by its own army as opposed to a Soviet-led invasion. But in 1989 the heroes of 1980 found themselves in power, in another extraordinarily peaceful and bloodless transition of power.

This is why our book has chosen Czechoslovakia and Poland, as opposed to the better-known and iconic fall of the Berlin Wall in 1989. Events in Berlin symbolised the overthrow of Communism to many in the West – and your author has his own piece of the Berlin Wall, hacked off personally, to prove it. But 1989 was a single event in Germany, with the only major protest movements having been suppressed a long time before. What made the Czechs and Poles special was the turning upside down of previous repression, of political prisoners becoming the new national leaders, of democracy triumphing over dictatorship. And historically that makes their two cases more interesting.

The easiest way to present the entries in this book is

chronologically. The significant starting point of each entry arranges the chapters. However a thematic look at the subjects is also possible:

Political protests
Non-violent protests
Boycotts
Strikes
Rock throwing, burning and violent protests
Marches and demonstrations
Pickets
Sit-ins and occupations
Civil disobedience

Many of these overlap, of course. Someone such as Gandhi used many types of protest. He was non-violent, but endorsed civil disobedience against the British. He was thoroughly political – agitating for Indian independence – and he organised a march to the sea to collect salt, while at the same time organising a boycott of British-made cotton.

But many protests come in single categories. And also this book has preferred items that recur. For example, the demonstrations in East Germany in 1989 led, as we shall see, to the fall of the iconic Berlin Wall. But our book looks at that in the context of the protests in Czechoslovakia, since what happened there in 1989, as well as being as important in its own way as the collapse of Communism in East Germany, was also a reversal of the attempt to introduce peaceful Communism – with a 'human face' – in 1968. The entry for Czechoslovakia looks at the events in both those years, and how what looked like a failure in 1968 turned unexpectedly to success and freedom in 1989.

So there are many recurrent themes in this book, with many entries embodying several of them at once.

Our book deals with so many contentious issues that we have to ask if there can ever be such a thing as true objectivity. Take genetically modified or GM crops – are they Frankenstein foods or science's answer to feeding millions of the starving in the Global South? There are equally zealous activists on both sides, each group utterly convinced of the entire correctness of their own particular cause. Anyone writing on such contemporary hot-button issues faces a real challenge! So your author hopes that this book has been as neutral as is possible, and one that enables readers to make their own minds up rather than telling them what they ought to be thinking.

Your author's two previous books in this series are about *past* conflicts: the battles of both the First World War and its successor the Second World War. The consequences of both conflicts are very much still with us – the Ukraine, the chaos in Syria, to name just two – but they are in the past. Many of the issues in this book are also historical. Women now have the same voting rights as men in Britain and the USA, trade unions are legal and India is not only an independent country but also one of the leading nations of the world.

But as a glance at those issues shows, much still has to be won. While women are enfranchised in Western democracies, for instance, there are other countries where they have no vote or any kind of rights at all. In some nations trade unions that exist independently of the government remain illegal, and workers have no genuine protection against those who exploit them. And while many parts of India are First World, part of the globally interconnected twenty-first century, other regions within that country have scarcely changed since the Middle Ages.

Some of the victories that have been won, and about which we read in this book, are in reality only partial, and that is something that those of us raised in the West need to remember. And events in the USA that occurred while this book was being written remind us – Martin Luther King achieved much, but are all African-Americans *truly* equal citizens of the USA? Again, there is much to ponder.

The two World Wars are thankfully over. They are truly *history*. But some of the issues raised here are profoundly *contemporary*. We do not yet know the ending. This is important. History written up until 1989–91 was composed *during* the Cold War, and as some of the entries in our book argue, those who predicted that conflict's demise were *very* few and far between. Therefore anything written in, say, 1979, would presuppose the continuation of the bipolar superpower conflict between the USA and USSR. The extraordinary events of 1989 in Poland and Czechoslovakia (at which we look) were unforeseeable *in 1979*, though in retrospect it is now easy to see where history was heading. Similarly, few in 2000 would have predicted that much of the beginning of the twenty-first century would be taken up with Islamic terrorism or wide-scale bloodshed across the Middle East. With several of the issues in our book we are therefore still in 1979 and the Cold War or 2000 and the Middle East, rather than looking back on something that is now over, such as World War II ending in

1945. We still do not have the perspective that history gives us.

So this book is a discussion starter, giving the outlines of some of the key protest movements of the past hundred or so years. Some of the movements we look at succeeded, others failed, yet others are still active. But many of them show that ordinary individuals, acting either alone or collectively, can move mountains. We may not be like idealistic young Oxford students in the 1970s, wearing dirty jerseys and asking a dictator to resign. But we can still try to make our world a better place. Hopefully this book can show us how to begin our journey.

SUFFRAGETTES AND VOTES FOR WOMEN

(1903–1920 and Beyond)

On December 5th 1908 the fiery Welsh radical David Lloyd George addressed a packed meeting, mainly female, in London's great Royal Albert Hall. The venue was full, since Lloyd George was also the new Chancellor of the Exchequer, the man in charge of the budget, and one of the most important politicians in Britain.

Many of his audience were *suffragists*, women who passionately supported the right of women to vote, but who rejected completely the campaign of the *suffragettes* to use violence and civil protest to bring attention to the cause. One of the suffragists in the audience was an intelligent Welsh schoolteacher, whose husband was Lloyd George's eye doctor. Also present and fearing trouble was their ten-year-old daughter, dreaming one day of becoming a medical student.

The child's worst fears were realised. Along with the suffragists who wanted to use argument and reason to further the goal of votes for women were numerous suffragettes who were looking for trouble. One of the latter, a woman named Helen Ogston, had come prepared. Over 70 suffragettes started to heckle David Lloyd George, and when the stewards tried to expel them, she brandished a whip! Eventually all the hecklers were removed and the Chancellor of the Exchequer – who supported votes for women – was able to finish his speech. But it turned out to be a very memorable and symbolic evening, one that the ten-year-old girl, who fulfilled her dream of being a doctor, could recall vividly for the remaining eighty-three years of her life. She was my grandmother, and as we shall see, it would take her another twenty years before she and my great-grandmother achieved the longed-for right to vote.

Slow but steady progress or the sudden use of violence to force the pace – this is always the dilemma of any protest movement. There is a division between those who favour a gradualist approach and those who want instant action by whatever means necessary, whether legal or not. This is a common thread through many of the protests we shall examine in this book, and the supporters of votes for women – the *suffrage*, to use the political term for voting rights – were no exception.

In our study we are looking at the past century or so, but the women's suffrage movement was the beneficiary of over a hundred previous years and more of the slow emancipation of the female half of the human species. In 1908, for instance, women in New Zealand had already enjoyed equal voting rights with men since 1893. However, in Switzerland it took decades more for women to be able to vote in federal elections. Not until 1971, in the lifetime of many of us today, did Swiss women get equal suffrage with men. By this time countries such as India, Israel and Sri Lanka had already had women serve as prime minister.

It is not just, therefore, in strongly patriarchal societies, such as in much of the Arab world, that women are still waiting. Indeed one should say that in many Muslim countries women have had the vote for decades, with female prime ministers or presidents in the world's largest Muslim nations such as Indonesia and Pakistan. In many regions the struggle for equal political rights is not history but an ongoing struggle against centuries of oppression and ill-treatment.

In the nineteenth century women in Britain had steadily accumulated a number of equal rights. A woman's property no longer automatically became her husband's upon marriage. Clever girls could go to university, and where my female ancestors attended, University College London, women not only received equal degrees to men (at Cambridge it was not until the 1940s that women became full graduates), but could study alongside them in subjects such as medicine. Women were slowly gaining the intellectual respect hitherto reserved for men. It was against this background, none of it associated with violence, that the suffragists began the campaign to get the vote for women. And one should remember that not all men could vote in, say, 1908 – many poor and socially disadvantaged working-class men did not possess the franchise either.

So when we think of the protest movements for female suffrage we must remember that there were two distinctive strands, each with a strategy of their own. And in addition, many men supported the suffragists, such as the future Labour Cabinet minister, Frederick Pethick-Lawrence, and indeed many members of the Liberal Cabinet, in power in Britain since December 1905.

The great Victorian intellectual John Stuart Mill, whose 1859 book *On Liberty* was one of the most significant works on that subject during that century, was a keen supporter of votes for women, advocating it as early as 1865–66. But it was not for another thirty years, until 1897, that the National Union of Women's Suffrage Societies (NUWSS) was formed. The leader of this was Millicent Fawcett, one of the founders of Newnham College in Cambridge (one of the first for women) and the sister of the distinguished medical pioneer Elizabeth Garrett Anderson. The NUWSS contained many women like this – intellectual, educated, middle class and with excellent social connections to the London political elite, not least to the Liberal Party, which won an electoral landslide over the Conservatives in the 1906 General Election.

However, this gradualist approach did not appeal to everyone, and in 1903 a Manchester widow called Emmeline Pankhurst founded her own group, the Women's Social and Political Union (WSPU). Her late husband Richard Pankhurst had long been a supporter of votes for women, and Pankhurst herself had close links with the then infant Labour Party and *its* founder, Keir Hardie. It was to this new group, the WSPU, that the *Daily Mail* gave the nickname that would stick: the '*suffragettes*'.

These campaigners spurned gradualism, and decided on the direct approach. As early as 1905 suffragettes were using militant tactics, smashing windows, demonstrating in public, setting fire to Royal Mailboxes and the like. In 1905 Christabel Pankhurst,

Emmeline's daughter, was imprisoned for such offences, and altogether well over a thousand women spent some time in jail for their militancy.

This was to cause no end of a problem to the Liberal government, some of whom supported the overall cause, but with plenty that did not. Psephologically, women in Britain have tended more to vote Conservative than Liberal and then Labour, so Liberals fearing votes for women were doing so on electoral grounds as well as out of misogyny.

Firstly, women wanted political prisoner status, which the government refused to grant them. Second, from 1909 onwards many started going on hunger strikes, a tactic that would increasingly be used in twentieth-century protests, from the peaceful Gandhi in India to the more violent IRA activists in Northern Ireland. Then, as now, those in power were reluctant to create martyrs, so one of the first suffragette hunger strikers, Marion Wallace Dunlop, was duly released after 91 days by a nervous government.

However, both sides realised that if women were automatically released, simply going on hunger strike would be an easy way for those imprisoned always to escape sentence. So in 1913 Reginald McKenna (Winston Churchill's successor as Home Secretary) introduced the Prisoners (Temporary Discharge for Ill Health) Act, popularly called the 'Cat and Mouse Act'. Once a hunger striker became dangerously emaciated and ill, she would be released, but re-imprisoned the moment her health restored itself on the outside. Already in 1909 violent force-feeding with tubes was often brought in, which sometimes caused much injury to those so treated.

Emmeline Pankhurst was a heroine for some women for her leadership of the struggle. For others she was a tyrant, since within WSPU circles her word was law. Some of her own family rebelled, notably Sylvia Pankhurst, one of the daughters. She became active in social work amidst the downtrodden and exploited of the East End of London, whether men or women. She enjoyed the family's ties with the growing Labour Party, which she saw as one of the best means of implementing a much wider social change than simply the issue of female suffrage. Christabel, by contrast, concentrated on the WSPU and the vote, spending some of her time beyond the reach of English law in Paris.

The anniversary of World War I has reminded us that in 1914 Britain was in a dangerously volatile political environment. Civil war was a real possibility in Ireland, with the Conservative Opposition at Westminster hideously close to a treasonous alliance with the Irish anti-independence Protestants. Labour relations were also bad, and the strife caused by suffragette militancy created much civil discord. But for the advent of war the situation could have become even more febrile, with catastrophic results for national stability.

As we know, the war brought its own disasters, with nearly a million slaughtered in the trenches of Flanders and elsewhere during 1914–1918.

Christabel Pankhurst became one of the war's most enthusiastic supporters, and many suffragettes decided to suspend the cause for the sake of patriotism and national unity.

And this brings us on to a natural question, posed by many historians ever since – such as by Trevor Lloyd in his book,

Suffragettes International. Did all the militancy help? Was violence worthwhile? Or did the aggressive tactics of the WSPU help indirectly? This issue is important, as it will apply elsewhere to many of the protests that are the subject of our book, as the same discussion comes up again and again.

In theory, women over thirty gained the vote in 1918 because of their splendid service to the nation during the war. Countless well-born women – such as, for example, the writer Vera Brittain – gave up their privileged lifestyle at home to serve as nurses at the Front. Countless poorer women became factory workers, especially in munitions, taking the place of men who had been sent to fight overseas.

But since the vote was for women *over* thirty, and with property qualifications, this meant in effect that the majority of women who had engaged in war service on the Home Front remained excluded from the vote. Either they were deemed too young (under thirty) or were of a lower social class (factory workers without property). Not until 1928 did women gain full electoral equality – the so-called 'flapper vote' – with *all* women over twenty-one being eligible to vote. And significantly, that right was given by the Conservative government of Stanley Baldwin, the prime minister and cousin of Rudyard Kipling.

So did the slow tactics of the NUWSS or the violence of the WSPU carry the day? Or was it simply the case that by 1918 politicians of all stripes finally realised that women deserved the vote? It is hard to say.

In concentrating, as many books and articles do, on the United Kingdom, we forget that similar struggles were taking place elsewhere, such as in the USA.

The notion of votes for women in the United States was debated back in the 1870s, and in 1869 the frontier state of Wyoming granted them the right to vote. As in Britain, women differed on how best to gain the suffrage, with the NAWSA (the National American Women's Suffrage Association) taking the more moderate stand. In contrast, the National Women's Party (NWP) advocated more militant tactics, with riots and picketing. One interesting observation is that one of the key NWP supporters and funders was Louisine Havemeyer, the widow of the rich sugar baron H. O. Havemeyer, and now herself one of the wealthiest women in the country. She is principally best known for the purchases that she and her husband made of Impressionist art, with a collection now mainly in the Metropolitan Museum in New York. But she was also an active suffragette, addressing the multitudes in Carnegie Hall and burning an effigy of the president, Woodrow Wilson. So while the names of Susan B. Anthony and of Sojourner Truth are those linked most strongly to the cause of women in the USA, it is interesting to reflect how wide their support was, from the very poor to the fabulously wealthy.

The Nineteenth Amendment to the US Constitution was ratified on August 18th 1920, when the support reached the necessary thirty-six states for the Amendment to become law. Significantly its wording, reflecting the federal nature of the USA, did not grant women the vote *directly* but rather proclaimed that no state should have a law that forbade them so to do. Certain states held out their ratification for some while after 1920, but in essence that vote enabled the majority of American women to exercise their franchise freely.

As we saw with the Swiss example, it took a while for other democracies to catch up. Nonetheless, the right to vote now became the democratic norm. However, many nations still hold out, and in much of the world women remain second-class citizens. The struggle is not yet over.

THE WOBBLIES AND EUGENE DEBS

(1894 and Beyond)

One of the many mysteries of American politics to outsiders is that there is no major equivalent of the Socialist or Labour parties of Europe and Britain and its Commonwealth, with political parties directly affiliated to the trade union movement. Democrats might have union links, but not in the same way as, say, Britain or France (where some unions used to have Communist ties instead).

However, historically this has not been the case. In the past there were Socialist candidates for the presidency, and trade unions that had overtly political links far further to the left than the Democratic Party.

The Industrial Workers of the World (IWW) or 'Wobblies', to use their nickname, were founded in the industrial unrest that existed in the American Midwest at the turn of the twentieth century, in 1905. In most of the Western world both then and today we had what are known as 'craft unions', which specialised according to the particular skill of the workers involved – the National Union of *Miners*, the *Transport* and General Workers Union, the Confederation of *Health Service* Employees etc. But what the Wobblies preferred was 'One Big Union' that represented all workers, regardless of speciality or trade. They preferred this arrangement for ideological reasons, in that the IWW existed to represent the working class as a social group, and the eventual overthrow of the capitalist system. It existed therefore not merely to represent workers in relation to management, but as an overtly *political* activist group.

As the mission statement document put it:

> The working class and the employing class have nothing in common . . . Between these two classes a struggle must go on until the workers of the world organise as a class, take possession of the means of production, abolish the wage system, and live in harmony with the Earth . . . Instead of the Conservative motto, 'A fair day's wage for a fair day's work,' we must inscribe upon our banner the revolutionary watchword, 'Abolition of the wage system . . .'

This was therefore more than normal trade union collective bargaining, it was a call to abolish the entire economic and political system upon which the USA and other capitalist countries were based. Needless to say, employers who might just about be able to tolerate wage bargaining by established unions found the Wobblies far beyond the acceptable pale.

The IWW approach was thus more similar in many ways to the anarchists and allied groups in countries such as Spain. Strikes and protests were the way in which to gain progress, and soon the Wobblies were active in many disputes. One of the early actions was a major industrial disruption in 1909 near Pittsburgh, Pennsylvania, in McKees Rock, at a railway car manufacturing plant. What began as a simple wage dispute soon developed into a massive confrontation between workers on the one hand, and police and private security guards on the other. Numbers are disputed, but between twelve and twenty-six were killed and many injured. The tactics of the managers, sending in strong-armed strike-breakers, were far more brutal than anything seen in Britain in, for example, strikes in coal mines in South Wales, at the same time.

By 1912 the Wobblies had over 25,000 members, and were involved in more than 150 strikes. It should be remembered, though, that mainstream organised labour in the USA was far bigger than this, and although the IWW stirred up much hostility and fear, they were still a minority overall. Many of their members were recent migrants to the United States, workers originating in Europe where conditions had often been harsher. Famously, many Wobblies were agricultural workers, formerly peasants in the more oppressive parts of the Old World. The Wheatland Hop Riot in 1913, in Yuba County California, was a similar incident of a pay dispute that escalated into violence, with four people killed and the IWW local leaders imprisoned unjustly for second-degree murder.

One of its dilemmas was how far the IWW should be affiliated to a political party, in this case the little-known and oft-forgotten Socialist Party in the USA. One of this party's key founders was the American socialist and thinker, Eugene V. Debs (1855–1926). Debs stood five times for the presidency of the USA, in 1900, 1904, 1908, 1912 and finally in 1920. Although he never came remotely near success, he is unique not just for the number of attempts but also from the fact that his final bid was from inside a prison cell.

Debs began as an orthodox trade unionist, working with the American Railway Union (ARU), and as a member of the Democratic Party. But in 1894 he was involved in major strike action with the new large-scale railway system in the USA, the Pullman Company. Workers at the Pullman factory lived in a company town south of Chicago. Pullman had raised workers' rents without raising their pay during a severe depression. The ARU signed up disgruntled workers who then staged a boycott refusing to run trains with Pullman cars. Within a few days 125,000 workers boycotted and the train system west of Detroit was crippled. Violence on both sides erupted. President Cleveland sent in 12,000 army troops to get the trains running again. Thirty workers were killed and more injured. By the end, 250,000 workers nationwide had joined the boycott. Debs was jailed for persisting in the strike despite court (and presidential) orders to the contrary. To calm things down, Cleveland rushed through legislation making Labor Day a national holiday only six days after the strike ended.

As often happens with freedom fighters, from Gandhi to Mandela and many before or since, what Debs read in jail transformed his life and thinking. Soon he was imbibing Marxist doctrine and rejecting Democratic politics for socialism. In particular he was attracted to the works of German-Czech socialist Karl Kautsky, a leading Marxist intellectual (and interestingly, after 1917, someone who rejected the Soviet version of Lenin and the Bolsheviks).

His first presidential attempt was not exactly a success – getting a mere 0.6% of the vote. His colleagues, as often happened with small revolutionary parties, were prone to splits, and in 1901 he joined a new group, the Social Democratic Party. Unlike later parties of the same name in Britain and Germany, this was strongly socialist/Marxist. But unlike in Europe, in the USA his remained very much a minority view, with one of his best vote counts being 913,693. This was nearly a million votes, but nowhere near electoral success.

In 1905 Debs was one of the founders of the IWW. But for many Wobblies, even the Socialists were incremental in their desire for revolutionary change, and the two organisations split. Many Socialists by contrast saw the IWW as nearer to anarchism than socialism. With this Debs reluctantly agreed.

His imprisonment in 1918, to no less than twenty years in jail, became a cause célèbre. His sentence was ostensibly under the Espionage Act, but in reality he was jailed for his implacable opposition to conscription and to American involvement in the First World War. After much dithering, President Wilson finally commuted the sentence in December 1921 and Debs was freed. He died in 1926, much mourned by socialists around the world.

But while his name lives on, his protest movement was not a success. The USA remains today one of the few Western nations without a strong and overtly *socialist* movement, a result, perhaps, of the strong doctrine of individualism on which it was founded.

Many of the issues involved in the story of Debs and of the IWW reveal the drawbacks of the confrontational stance of the Wobblies. In addition, their refusal to agree with collective bargaining or with contracts of any kind played both into the hands of management and also those of the more regular trade unions. One example is that in Lawrence, Massachusetts, in 1912, often nicknamed the 'Bread and Roses Strike' because it concerned mainly women textile workers. This strike featured the first moving picket line in the USA. Although short-term the Wobblies were successful, long-term it is argued that because the IWW rejected contracts in the name of class war, the management were able to batter down organised resistance. Most of the workers left the Wobblies as an inevitable result.

Wobblies attracted violence. In November 1916 police shot five IWW members dead on a steamboat in Washington State (with six more possibly being drowned). Then, when the USA entered World War I in 1917, the refusal of Wobblies to agree to conscription made their activity illegal. While not all Wobblies endorsed this view, it gave the American government the excuse needed to suppress IWW activity. Several Wobblies were jailed, often harshly.

Soon the IWW began to peter out, its membership declining. The coming to power of the Bolsheviks in the USSR scared many Americans, and the Wobblies, although perhaps closer to Spanish anarchism in many ways than totalitarian Soviet Communism, were inevitably tarred with their brush. The IWW continued to limp on – taking part, for instance, in some of the protests connected to the 1960s counterculture – but they were far smaller than ever before. The union exists today, not just in the USA but also in several other countries. However, its main days are over.

CHURCHILL AND THE
TONYPANDY RIOTS

(1910)

In most of the world – especially perhaps the United States –
Winston Churchill is regarded as one of the greatest statesmen
of all time, the man whose action and oratory saved Britain from
Nazi invasion and tyranny in 1940.

However, in large parts of South Wales he is a villain, not
a hero, for decisions that he took thirty years before his heroic
defence of the United Kingdom and our democratic way of life
in the Second World War. In fact, his actions during a coal strike
in 1910 nearly cost him the premiership in 1940, with what
would have been disastrous consequences for the struggle against
Fascism.

Until recent years the predominant way of life in South
Wales was industrial heavy labour, whether in the coal mines

of the Rhondda Valley or the steelworks in areas nearby. Before the mines were taken into public ownership in the 1940s they were private companies owned often by absentee landlords frequently motivated more by the profit line than by the welfare of their workers. In 1910 some of the miners, in the region of Tonypandy, made the bold move of requesting more pay. This the owners would not contemplate, and in September of that year the proprietors of the local pits locked out the workers. Since this was in an era before the welfare benefits of today, this caused immense hardship.

Some of the miners rioted in protest. Normally such matters would be dealt with by the local police, but since the constabulary in Glamorganshire were hard-pressed because of industrial unrest elsewhere, they were unable to deal with the protests on their own.

Then, as now, only the Home Secretary in London could deal with any national police requests. In late 1910 the Home Secretary was Winston Churchill, widely regarded at the time as being on the radical, politically progressive wing of the Liberal government. He was reluctant to escalate the situation but agreed that police from other areas of the United Kingdom could be employed, and, if absolutely necessary, the military as well.

Britain is traditionally a country that does not like to employ the armed services in civil disputes. When this has happened, such as in the early nineteenth century, at St Peter's Field in the north of England, it has caused both carnage and profound controversy. Such would now prove to be the case in South Wales. Churchill was well aware of this. What happened next is a classic example of how difficult it is to write completely objective history. The events that unfolded have gone down in legend and folklore in the mining communities of South Wales, meaning that the tales have often been exaggerated in the telling.

Churchill's actual role in the saga remains a topic of controversy.

At the start of November the miners – the South Wales Miners' Federation – decided to launch a formal strike. Since this involved the picketing of several workplaces, the tensions escalated and the local authorities feared that the situation would get out of hand. So by most accounts, it was the decision-takers in *local* government rather than the government some distance away in London that actually wanted troops to be employed against the miners.

On November 8th local miners reacted violently against the colliery owners' decision to employ strike-breakers. Civil disturbance erupted and the police – who now included many policemen from outside Wales – felt unable to control the turmoil.

The 18th Hussars were not far from Tonypandy, so on the night of November 9th they charged into the riots in order to suppress them. What happened next has been widely disputed for well over a century! It is unquestionable that many miners were injured, and not a few police as well. While one miner almost certainly died of his wounds, there is no consensus on whether or not people were killed by the cavalry charges. Whatever the truth might be, the strike was effectively over, the miners lost and many of them were imprisoned for rioting.

Churchill's defenders would argue that there is a huge difference between *allowing* the possibility of cavalry to be used and actually issuing a direct order for their use. Unfortunately for his reputation, the latter interpretation is the one that has gone down the years in the history of South Wales, in the mining communities around Britain and in the folklore of the Labour Party. This is why in 1940 there were some in that party who were reluctant to see Churchill become prime minister of a wartime coalition government in which Labour would play a major role.

Thankfully for democracy and the struggle for survival against Hitler, wiser counsels prevailed and the Labour leadership fully endorsed Churchill's premiership, with the results that we all know. But differing interpretations of who ordered the cavalry against ordinary strikers nearly derailed British history decades after the events involved.

After 1945 the Labour Party took power and nationalised the coal industry. But as we shall see, that did not solve the long-term problem of industrial relations in British collieries, in Wales and elsewhere. And in the 1970s and 1980s it became a truly national issue.

CONSCIENTIOUS OBJECTORS

(1914–1973)

A *conscientious objector* is someone who is against war, and therefore refuses to fight in the armed services of their country. Since women are not usually conscripted, this in essence means anti-war *men*, though there are of course exceptions. Israel is the best-known exception, and Norway the most recent, in drafting women as well as men.

According to Article 18 of the UN Convention on Human Rights, passed not long after the Second World War (and ratified in different forms with new but similar treaties since then):

Everyone has the right to freedom of thought, conscience and religion; this right includes freedom to change his religion or belief, and freedom, either alone or in community with others and in public or private, to manifest his religion or belief in teaching, practice, worship and observance.

While this seems to relate more to religious rights than to the freedom to choose not to fight in war, in practice many pacifists, those against war, have a religious origin of their beliefs. In the eighteenth century this applied to the Quakers (also known as the 'Society of Friends'), and to the Mennonites, whose pacifism stems back to the time of the Reformation in the sixteenth century. Later on, other groups, such as Jehovah's Witnesses and Seventh Day Adventists, joined the list of those for whom religious belief made active war service on the battlefield morally impossible for their free exercise of conscience.

The important thing to note is that for there to be conscientious objection, there has to be a military conscription against which to exercise one's conscience. So there is an important difference between just being against war, or a particular war, and actual full-blown conscientious objection. The million or more who marched in London and in other parts of Britain in 2003 to protest against British involvement in the war in Iraq may well, in many cases, have been pacifists who would have been opposed to *any* war. But there were others who were simply against *that* war, for personal or political as well as moral reasons. For our purposes such protest, however legitimate, does not count. In Britain since the late 1950s there has been no conscription or any kind of military draft in the United Kingdom. So in 2003, when war with Iraq began, none of the protesters in Trafalgar Square were liable to be sent at any time to fight in Iraq in a war with whose basic premises they disagreed. The British Armed Forces have, for well over half a century now, been entirely volunteer forces, with no citizen legally obliged to join any of them or be compelled to fight at home or abroad.

So being a CO – or 'conchie' to use the slightly insulting term sometimes employed – means an objector not merely against war but also someone opposed to being compelled to join the armed services of their own nation. Britain was unusual in being a major military power without conscription, and the few years after World War II in which it continued to have a conscript army even in peacetime was very much an exception to the volunteer rule.

British generals and others have also tended to think that volunteer soldiers fight better than conscripts. That might be a controversial view but it is the notion that has tended historically to prevail. We forget that the great Duke of Wellington's troops at Waterloo were not only in the majority *non*-British, but they were also volunteers. The same applied to the brave 'Pals Battalions' of World War I, friends from the same village or tennis club or factory or cricket team who joined up together in the rush of patriotism in 1914. All of them were volunteers, and it was a *volunteer* not a conscript British army that was wiped out on the first day of the Battle of the Somme in 1916.

In fact it was the scale of losses, of deaths in the trenches, that persuaded a hitherto reluctant British government to introduce conscription at all. That lasted until 1920, and it was back to a volunteer army until 1939, when, with the threat of war with Nazi Germany becoming inevitable, peacetime conscription was brought in for the first time ever in British history. It was the switch from hot war 1939–1945 to cold war after 1945, and the fear of both the Soviet menace in Europe and the need to suppress colonial troubles in places such as Malaya, that led to compulsory military enlistment being prolonged until 1960, disguised in the term 'National Service'.

In the First World War COs had a very hard time, and were often maltreated or not taken seriously. Wanting to avoid the carnage of the trenches was naturally understandable, but genuine objection was frequently dismissed out of hand.

And here it is important to distinguish between the various kinds of objection. Some were absolutists, who refused to do anything at all. Such people, while usually internally consistent morally in their world view, were seldom heard sympathetically. Others were prepared to do peaceful alternative service, such as working as ambulance drivers, stretcher-bearers (something that was highly dangerous, being under enemy gunfire) or agricultural workers, taking the place of farm labourers who had chosen to go to the Front. This was not absolute refusal, but a kind of protest all the same. People prepared to undertake such work were usually treated more sympathetically, as they were prepared in some way or another to do something for their country in the hour of grave need.

World War One also saw many men – usually privates or NCOs, since officers had social connections to help them – shot for what was then called cowardice, but which we would today regard as shell shock. This proved very controversial then, as it has been ever since. But by 1939 views had changed very considerably, COs were taken seriously and those wanting to do some alternative to fighting were often given their wish, though by no means everyone. Then, in 1960, the very last young men were conscripted. After 1963 the British armed services switched to being entirely voluntary, which they have been ever since. No British civilian was forced to be in Northern Ireland, Bosnia, Kosovo, Afghanistan or Iraq. Interestingly, the esteem in which Britain's armed services are held today by ordinary people has seldom been higher, as organisations such as Hope for Heroes testify.

Many other major countries, including those today such as Russia that still have the draft, have believed to the contrary. For them, COs have a major problem, since fighting for your nation is regarded as patriotism and refusing so to do is often misinterpreted as either cowardice or treachery or both. In places such as Turkey or Russia the right of conscientious objection is recognised in theory only and in practice by imprisonment or perhaps worse.

A country that had the draft for military service well into peacetime is the United States. This entry will concentrate on the pre-Vietnam experience.

The USA traditionally did not force its citizens into uniform. No one was obliged to fight Native Americans out West or to invade Mexico. But there was one major exception to this – the American Civil War, 1861–1865. Both sides needed as many soldiers as possible for victory. Not only that, but it was necessary for self-defence, especially in the Confederate states in the South as the Union armies of the North began their inexorable conquest of the rebels. It was 'fighting for Dixie' and for the values involved, not just fighting in any old war.

With the First World War, however, things were different.

Many in the now reunited USA did not see why they should fight in conflicts involving disputes thousands of miles away, and in many cases, involving countries and empires from which they or their parents had fled to start life in the New World. The draft proved necessary when the number of those volunteering proved minuscule in comparison to the large numbers needed to field the American Expeditionary Force as an effective fighting body in Europe.

Exemptions were granted for religious groups traditionally opposed to war – such as the Mennonites – but the downside for many was that mainstream denominations that did not have this stand (such as Catholics, Baptists, Episcopalians etc.) were expected to fight. Groups needed for the Home Front, such as farmers, were also exempted.

First time around, the USA did not need to extend conscription beyond 1918 as the war ended that year. The Supreme Court ruled that the draft was legal, thereby criminalising those such as the 'Wobblies' ideological opponents of war (dealt with in that entry).

In 1940 it became evident that another war was coming whether the USA wished it or not, and as is now widely known, isolationist opinion in the United States remained strong. But the mighty USA had an army only the same size as that of Belgium! So selective conscription was reintroduced, with a draft regime that lasted down to 1947.

The American government was clear in distinguishing between those who opposed *any* war, and those against that *particular* war, with the former looked upon more favourably as being principled objectors to armed conflict in general. They were also more kindly disposed to those willing to do alternative work, as was the case with Britain above, such as ambulance driving, agricultural labour and the like. By and large it was those who refused to do *anything* who were treated ruthlessly and sent to work camps, rather than those against violence but patriotically happy to help their country in a peaceful manner.

What is unusual about the USA is that it effectively extended the draft beyond 1947 down to the last group enlisted in 1973 (with conscription therefore ending in practice by 1975). Conscription lasted so long because of the Cold War, but it was also very controversial, since it was an extension of conscription well into peacetime. A lottery system was used – a good number and it could be cushy service in Germany or Japan, a bad number and it could be front line service in harm's way in Korea or, later on, in Vietnam. Thousands of men enlisted voluntarily in order to have some leeway in where they were posted: often such people, especially if they were university graduates, were able to become officers and serve in safe berths such as military intelligence, where they were in uniform but not in danger of being killed in combat.

It was this system that operated during the Vietnam War, which, as we see in the entry on that conflict, proved to be exceptionally controversial. But thousands of others were lucky, going to Europe, for example, learning languages or technical skills, and with the benefits of being veterans able to get good jobs on the basis of the free training they had received while enlisted. And as it was lottery-based, your fate – extreme danger in Vietnam, friendly folk and good beer in Germany – was literally the luck of the draw.

With the end of the American active military engagement in Vietnam, the draft, by now almost toxic, was abolished. The USA has fought in countless wars since then, from Afghanistan to Iraq, but with a *volunteer* army, navy and air force.

However, in places as varied as Russia and Israel, conscription continues, and in the former case often in harsh circumstances. In these countries COs are not treated as leniently or with understanding, and the problem of conscientious objection or protest to military service remains.

GANDHI AND NON-VIOLENCE

(1930: and 1893–1948)

One of the most important people to have lived in the twentieth century was the outstanding Indian leader and apostle of non-violence, Mohandas Karamchand Gandhi, usually known by the honorific *Mahatma* Gandhi (or Great Soul) and to his followers as 'Bapu' or father, 1869–1948.

Gandhi is a true icon of our time, one of the religious leaders most revered even in today's secular age. Ironically, in the twenty-first century he is possibly more appreciated *outside* India than inside it. Today's government is that of the BJP, whose path to independence was not Gandhi's, and a member of whose militant wing, the RSS (or National Volunteer Association), was Gandhi's assassin. In the West, Gandhi is increasingly looked to as a modern saint, since his influence on other giants of recent history, such as Martin Luther King in the USA and Nelson Mandela in South Africa, both came to take the non-violent approach that Gandhi embodied.

He was very nearly not a hero of any kind at all. He was born into an upper-middle-class background, qualified as a barrister in London at the Inner Temple, and when he went to South Africa to practise law he dressed very much as a proper gentleman. But London had its effect – he began the frugal lifestyle for which he became famous, met radical English people through his embracement of vegetarianism, and read eagerly the teachings of Jesus in the Sermon on the Mount. While Gandhi remained a loyal and devout Hindu – perhaps too much a devotee for later Muslims – he was eclectic in his religious views and happy to absorb Christian teachings where he felt that they fitted in to the world view that he proclaimed.

He lived in South Africa for twenty-one years: 1893–1914. It was being thrown out of a train in 1893, simply for being a non-white, that began the process of radicalisation that made him the eminent figure for which we revere him today. His protest against racial discrimination, and the non-violent way in which he resisted the many injustices of the colonial authorities, was the spark that lit the flame of his later work in India.

And one thing is important to remember. At the same time that Gandhi was protesting against the British in South Africa, just a few miles away in German South-West Africa (today's Namibia) the Germans were massacring as many as 100,000 Herero tribespeople for daring to dissent from colonial rule. Had Gandhi been under German rule he would not simply have been arrested 250 times, he would have been shot and we would never have heard of him. Gandhi was fortunate in that while the British were not perfect – the hideous carnage at Amritsar in 1919 shows that – by and large they did not believe in the mass murder of their opponents. When we think of what Gandhi's non-violence achieved we should remember that his opponents were opposed to the use of violent suppression for most of the time.

By 1906 he had decided on a life of celibate action, as his biographer Judith Brown has put it, 'to free himself to care for the whole of humanity . . .' His ascetic way of living now became his norm, and it is interesting that his community in South Africa was called 'Tolstoy Farm', after the Russian thinker and writer Leo Tolstoy, whose simple lifestyle inspired Gandhi so much. (The celibate option much upset his poor wife Kasturba! She was also not happy about the caste pollution involved in actions such as toilet cleaning. Nor did Gandhi's children fully appreciate their father's choices. Sometimes greatness comes with a price at home . . .)

By the time he returned to India in 1914 he had worked out his philosophy. There were, biographers tell us, two core pillars: *satya* or truth, and *ahimsa* or non-violence. It is easy to remember the second, but to Gandhi truth was very strongly as important. As Judith Brown puts it, 'if truth was the goal, then non-violence was inevitably the means'. To him, his means of protest against injustice or British oppression was *satyagraha* or 'truth force', and being active but without violence was not so much weakness as the projection of inner strength.

(As his life progressed, his ways of gaining inner strength, such as sleeping naked but asexually with young women, was to cause huge controversy and much misunderstanding. His followers in the Indian independence movement, such as Pandit Nehru and V. J. Patel, did not always appreciate his lifestyle, as it looked as eccentric then as it does now. And while Gandhi believed in many roads to God, and in religious toleration, the Hindu nature of his religious practice was distinctly alienating to the Muslim community and their leaders, such as Muhammad Ali Jinnah. Gandhi was unquestionably sincere, but not always easy to follow.)

In 1909 he had written a major work, *Hind Swaraj*, which advocated independence for India, so when he returned home to the subcontinent in 1914 he was already a hero. Many of his lifestyle choices were also political. Take the famous symbol of the spinning wheel – now in the Indian flag. This is a *charka* and the key thing about it is that it is the *Indian* way of making things. For a long time India had been devastated by the rise of the cotton industry in Britain: wearing *local* homespun, or *khadi*, hit directly and in a non-violent way at British oppression. *Swadeshi*, the making of products in *India*, was an excellent way of combating the Raj.

This was, though, a thoroughly old-fashioned India, that of the village commune. For pro-independence protesters, such as the Cambridge-educated Pandit Nehru, this was the very opposite of the dynamic and thoroughly modern India that many of the younger members of the Indian National Congress wanted to create. Not a few Indians, such as the increasingly unhappy Congress leader Subhas Chandra Bose, doubted that *non*-violence would work – Bose would later lead an army against the Raj in collaboration with the Japanese during World War

11. For the RSS, the semi-military organisation of independence activists, the passive resistance of Gandhi and his kind was not enough to get rid of the British. And the RSS, then as now in our own time, was aggressively Hindu – or *Hindutva*, wanting to see India as a wholly *Hindu* nation with no room for the Muslim, Jain or Christian minorities. We forget in making Gandhi into a hero that there were alternative ways of planning for the future. While Gandhi wished to include Muslims within the Congress fold, Jinnah and other Muslims began to fear what a majority Hindu country might be like for those outside the fold.

Gandhi, as his biographers remind us, was more of a force than a formal player – while he held huge influence in Congress, he was often not an official leader, but a powerful moral influence. He was, though, the chief campaigner in some of the major anti-British protests, in 1920–1922, then again in 1930–1934, and finally during the Second World War, a conflict into which Britain propelled India without due consultation with the Indian people themselves.

One of the problems that the Indian protesters faced was the fact that the British were themselves divided, not just on whether or not to give India its independence, but if it were to be given its freedom, how fast progress to such a goal should be. In both 1919 and in 1935, Acts of Parliament were passed that gave far greater autonomy to India than had existed before. In the 1930s one of the most zealous opponents of giving even the most basic political self-government to India was Winston Churchill, who referred to Gandhi with deliberate insult as a 'half-naked fakir' and whose resolute blocking of Indian independence during 1940–1945 infuriated not just Indians but the Americans as well.

In turn, some Indians agreed with collaboration with the British Raj, in order better to train for full freedom when it came. Such people were naturally wary of Gandhi, and because of his status are often airbrushed out of the story.

Nevertheless Gandhi's campaigns did make some difference. The Salt March of 1930 is a classic example. That year the Indian National Congress declared that India should be independent. Gandhi saw that the British Raj had given itself a monopoly on salt. So he and a band of followers marched all the way (some 240 miles) from his ashram to the sea, where they proceeded, illegally, to make salt. Gandhi and some of his followers were immediately arrested. But soon the British found that Gandhi in jail was far more trouble than as a free man. So they released him in order to engage in talks with the then viceroy, Lord Irwin. In fact, not long later the government in Britain began to realise that it was time to prepare India for eventual independence, and, as we have just seen, did all possible to implement such a process whatever the ferocious opposition in London of Winston Churchill. Gandhi was himself invited to London and took part in direct round-table talks with the government itself. He also visited the East End of London and Balliol College Oxford, the college at which so many viceroys of India had been educated. His visit created a sensation wherever he travelled and to many he was now a hero, in Britain as well as at home. So *maybe* Gandhi's salt march made a difference? Historians disagree.

In September 1939, when Britain went to war with Germany, the then Viceroy Lord Linlithgow declared India at war, but without consulting the Congressional leaders first. As a result, all

Congress Party members resigned from their elected government posts, and began the 'Quit India' movement. It should be said that many, such as Nehru, realised full well that a Japanese conquest of India would be far worse, as was justified by the barbaric treatment that Japan meted out to its newly captured territories from 1940–41 onwards. Nonetheless, the widespread civil disobedience campaign that now began created gigantic headaches for the British colonial authorities, and many troops were used to suppress dissent rather than fight the Japanese invaders.

When the Labour Party took office in 1945, official British policy was to grant India its independence as soon as possible. But the delays under Churchill had given the Muslim League and its leader, Jinnah, time in which to create an alternative scenario, one in which the two majority Muslim parts of India were to be separated off to create a new nation called Pakistan. (In 1971 East Pakistan became Bangladesh.) This was profoundly upsetting to Gandhi, who had wanted the entire Raj to stay together as one united country. There was large-scale intercommunal rioting and people were killed, as the British insisted both on keeping to the tight timetable while at the same time fulfilling the Herculean task of working out where the partition lines should be placed now that Pakistan was to be separate from India. Some of the worst carnage was in what was then a still united Bengal (now West Bengal in India and Bangladesh as a country on its own). Gandhi went bravely to Calcutta, to embark on a hunger strike for peace. While this helped ameliorate the situation somewhat, it did not end the violence altogether. When in August 1947 India gained its independence, so too did Pakistan, much to Gandhi's disappointment. Millions were killed or injured as Hindus fled from Pakistan and Muslims from India.

On January 30th 1948 Gandhi was assassinated in Delhi, by Nathuram Godse, a member of the aggressively Hindu RSS, which we met earlier. If the RSS had sought to get rid of Gandhi, the effect of his death was the opposite, turning him into an icon, a martyr and an object of national veneration.

However, although he continues to be hero-worshipped today across the world, his slightly quaint and old-fashioned ideas of how a modern Indian state should be run made him more revered than followed. The industrial nation of India today is not one he would have recognised. As we saw earlier, today it is the political wing of the RSS, the BJP, that controls India. But as the embodiment of non-violence, of a different way of protest, he is still a role-model for millions, even if they are outside India rather than in it. His dream lives on.

NAZI BOOK BURNINGS

(1933)

The city of Berlin, now once again the German capital, is full of ghosts, and not just from the Communist era when the place was divided, but also from its far more evil and Nazi past. The Third Reich thankfully lasted a mere twelve years rather than the thousand dreamt of by Hitler, its creator, but the lessons of those dreadful dozen years are with us still. Once again the Jews are being singled out and used as scapegoats by those with malign intent, and free speech is under attack again, as it always has been in totalitarian societies of whatever stripe or with ideologies for whom it poses a threat.

For centuries there was an *Index of Forbidden Books* that censored what people were allowed to read. During the Communist era in the USSR, and then wider afield in Soviet bloc countries and in China, even to read a particular book or author could be a highly subversive act. In our own lifetime writers, thinkers and playwrights have been forced underground, imprisoned, even executed, for daring to think their own thoughts. In many parts of the world today freedom of expression is banned by the authorities and artistic or literary freedom outlawed, as artists and novelists in recent days in China have discovered.

When we study the Nazi period there is always the danger that we make it uniquely dreadful, and think it so especially terrible that it could never occur again. But in fact, as many millions were slaughtered under other regimes in the twentieth century as were obliterated by the Third Reich. Hitler's monstrosity was his own but he did not possess a monopoly of evil.

Nevertheless, as the book and television series *The Nazis: A Warning from History* reminds us, even the most outwardly civilised of people can be deceived into supporting an utterly disgusting and vile ideology. In many of the entries in this book students appear as either people of the progressive left, or as idealists with beliefs that put them on the good side of history rather than on the bad – although much of that sentence depends upon your own political point of view . . . However this is by no means always the case. Students are like ordinary people everywhere and can be just as prone to the dark side as well as to that of virtue. And in the 1930s the *German Students Union* proved that beyond doubt, by their active support for the Nazi book burning and censorship programme not long after Hitler's accession to power in 1933.

Many of Germany's greatest writers had been Jewish or held views sympathetic to Jewish people. Others were socialists or Communists, and therefore ideologically unacceptable to a totalitarian world view such as that espoused by the Nazis. Therefore in the new mindset, embodied by Joseph Goebbels, the Propaganda Minister of the Third Reich, they had to be destroyed, *forbidden*.

(And interestingly, the words of a present-day terrorist group, Boko Haram, mean in English: Western education is *forbidden* . . . There is a massive difference between a militant army in part of West Africa in the twenty-first century and the Nazi regime in 1930s Germany, but there are parallels which are surely of significance upon which we can reflect today?)

So when the Nazis seized power in January 1933 they started actively to use propaganda to achieve permanent rule and get rid of democracy. One of their most active wings had been their youth movement – now to become compulsory for all German children to join – and many of these young people had gone on to study at university. It was to such Nazi students that the leadership now turned.

Germany had been world famous for the glories of its literature and for the strength of its scientific discovery. One of the many countless results of twelve years of Nazi rule in Germany is that it went from being one of the most advanced scientific nations in the world to just another country, with the USA (and to a lesser extent Britain as well) taking up the mantle. Why? The answer is that numerous Nobel Prize-winning scientists were Jews, and they were not welcome in the new deliberately *Judenfrei* (or Jewish-free) Reich.

Many great German authors were long dead, but their books remained in libraries across the country. Berlin had long enjoyed one of the greatest literary collections, and this soon concerned Goebbels and his henchmen.

In the past people had been burnt at the stake, and the Nazis were to murder millions of people in all kinds of ways in the years ahead. Ideas cannot be so treated, but you can burn the books in which they are contained. In past centuries heretical books had been treated in this manner, and so the Nazis, in collaboration with their sympathisers in the German Students Union, now chose to rid the nation of its pre-Nazi past.

Therefore they decided upon book burnings, with the biggest one in Berlin on May 10th 1933. Thousands of precious volumes, the cream of centuries of German literature, some of the most noble thoughts ever put to paper, were piled high near the university, and set alight in a gigantic bonfire.

What follows is just an extract. In reading it, ask if there are similar people today who also hold his views, even though coming to such opinions from different directions:

The era of extreme Jewish intellectualism has come to an end and the German revolution has again opened the way for the true essence of being German. This revolution was not started at the top, it burst forth from the bottom, upwards. It is, therefore, in the very best sense of the word, the expression of the will of the Volk. There stands the worker next to the bourgeois, student next to soldier and young worker, here stand the intellectuals next to the proletariat.

During the past fourteen years while you, students, had to suffer in silent shame the humiliations of the November Republic [i.e. the Weimar Republic], your libraries were inundated with the trash and filth of Jewish 'asphalt' literati.

While scholarship gradually isolated itself from real life, the young Germany has re-established new conditions in our legal system and normalised our life.

New research about Nazi Germany has shown that while many ordinary Germans did support the new ideology there were plenty who did not. But such was the sheer violence of the Nazi state that protest against the protests was a highly dangerous act. The first inhabitants of the concentration camps were often socialists, trade unionists and other political opponents of Nazism, as well as the Jewish prisoners about whom we know so much today. Many Germans were horrified at this act of cultural vandalism, but they were too afraid to speak. And as the old saying goes, all that is necessary for evil people to prevail is for good people to do nothing. Speaking out against the Nazis was of course a very dangerous and brave thing to do. But we are all very aware in our own time of the consequences of silence.

Today we live in an era where free speech can still cost you your life and in which Jews can be murdered just as they were in the 1930s. The murderers are no longer Nazis and the rationale has changed, but could we say that the principle is the same? In 1933 not enough people around the world said '*Je suis juif*' and we know what happened then . . .

THE JARROW MARCH

(1936)

The Great Depression of the 1930s hit working people hard all over the Western world, as manufacturing slumped to all-time low levels. Towns that had once been prosperous became shadows of their former selves and workers who had enjoyed what they thought would be employment for life discovered that in the new economic climate jobs could vanish overnight.

Some of the protests against unemployment, and against the uncaring attitude of national governments, captured the popular imagination. One such event was that of the marchers from the industrial town of Jarrow, in the north-east of England, in October 1936.

That particular region has long been famous for shipbuilding, ever since the nineteenth century. The ships built there were originally a reflection of the maritime nature of Britain. This was a country whose Royal Navy ruled the waves and a nation that depended on free trade and exports around the world. Until the First World War began in 1914 shipping made the United Kingdom the number one global power.

Jarrow, during this period, was a town of prosperity and high employment. But as the Great Depression took hold, the days of plenty ended, and many of the biggest shipyards either had to reduce their workforce, or close altogether, as order books declined. Jarrow was badly affected and by 1936 well over 70% of the former workers were unemployed.

Unemployment benefit was not as adequate then as it is now, and no National Health Service existed either – all medicine was costly. The workers became desperate to gain the widest audience for their plight. In Ellen Wilkinson, their Member of Parliament, they had a doughty champion, and together they came up with a plan that would, without their realising it at the time, enter national folklore.

They decided to *march* the entire distance from Jarrow to London, a distance of nearly 300 miles. This they did, some 207 of them, and drew attention to their cause all the way on the long journey south.

In the short term the march was a failure. Nothing happened when they reached London, other than the popular attention in the press given to those who had taken so dramatic a step to publicise their plight. None of them gained jobs and Jarrow remained stricken until the advent of the Second World War. In September 1939, three years later, the urgent military need to build ships became paramount and money was no longer an object. But the idea of ordinary working people taking the initiative for themselves, walking great distances and bringing the concerns of the north-east down to London, had the effect on the imagination for which they had hoped. With the advent of the Labour government in 1945 – of which Ellen Wilkinson became the Minister for Education – the conditions that they faced in the 1930s were abolished. Today the same region is still struggling with the effects of another recession, and shipbuilding is no longer the money-spinner it had been in its nineteenth-century heyday. But the Jarrow Marchers have never been forgotten.

CND AND THE GREENHAM WOMEN

(1948–1983)

Did nuclear war ever happen? Why did millions of American schoolchildren in the 1950s have to practise hiding under their desks, in air raid attack drills? Or thousands of homes in Western Europe have to put food supplies in their cellars in case supplies broke down after a nuclear first strike?

Thankfully, the much-feared nuclear Armageddon never took place or we would not be here today. Hiding under a desk would in any case never have saved anyone from acute radiation poisoning, and food in the cellars would have been contaminated by anyone saving it. But so terrible a conflict might well have happened at any time during the long Cold War, from the origins of that conflict in the 1940s to the demise of the Soviet Union in 1991. One of the USA's leading historians of this period, John

Lewis Gaddis, has written a book with the fitting title of *We Now Know*. As he reminds us, in the post-Cold War world in which we live now, the nightmare never happened. Those thinkers, like the British former Bletchley Park code-breaker Sir Harry Hinsley, who argued that the *possession* of nuclear weapons, rather than giving them up, actually prevented nuclear Armageddon instead of causing it, were *in the end* proved to be right.

But throughout the Cold War, say from 1948 (the Communist takeover of Czechoslovakia) down to 1989 and the fall of the Berlin Wall and the ultimate demise of the Soviet Union in 1991, millions of us in the West lived in daily existential fear of a nuclear attack on our country. For if it had actually happened, the fallout would have slaughtered millions of innocent civilians in a carnage that would have made even the 80 million deaths of the Second World War seem small in comparison. In fact, so bad could a nuclear conflagration have become that the two superpowers (the USA and USSR) could not only have destroyed each other – mutually assured destruction (MAD) – but also have wiped life itself out altogether in a nuclear winter. The dust clouds formed by so many nuclear explosions and the fallout could in a short time have blotted out the light from the sun and extinguished all forms of life left on earth.

However, neither nuclear winter nor MAD ever happened. In retrospect this is because both the superpowers knew that they could obliterate one another, and, being what international relations specialists call 'rational actors', they never launched an attack that would end humankind. The Hinsley theory, that deterrence works, proved correct.

But for over forty years we did not know that. All it would

have needed was some American or Soviet leader to become ever so slightly *irrational* and launch Armageddon in a moment of madness, and human civilisation as we know it would have vanished for ever.

One of the most famous instances during which World War III *might* have happened was in November 1983, something revealed recently in television documentaries and then online. This was an innocent North Atlantic Treaty Organisation training exercise, of the kind that happened all the time during the Cold War. On this occasion it was code-named *Able Archer*. It had been decided by NATO to simulate what would happen during a nuclear stand-off that led to actual war breaking out, a wise precaution given the extreme results of a real war happening by mistake.

Unfortunately the Soviets had, since 1981 and Ronald Reagan's election to the White House, become paranoid that the West *would* launch a nuclear strike against the Soviet bloc. So when the NATO exercises began, the USSR started to believe its own myth and feared that this *was* the start of World War III.

Thankfully the KGB had a spy in the West who assured them that *Able Archer* was only an exercise, and the MI6 spy working for the British, Oleg Gordievsky, was able to explain the reason behind Soviet paranoia to *his* contacts. Everyone realised that the fear had been for nothing, but as experts have rightly commented, the November 1983 misunderstanding took the world as close to nuclear war as any confrontation since the Cuban Missile Crisis back in the 1960s. Only now, with the declassification of *Able Archer*, do we know how near we all came to extinction as a human race in 1983.

The Cuban Crisis, in October 1962, was started by the decision of the Soviet government to station nuclear missiles in Cuba, which is not far from the southern part of the American mainland, in Florida. Europeans were used to the presence of such weapons near their homes, but to the USA it was a major shock. President Kennedy displayed brinkmanship, which came scarily close, during the worst of the thirteen-day crisis, to actually starting a nuclear exchange. In the end the USSR blinked first, withdrew its missiles from Cuba in return for the USA withdrawing a similar arsenal from Turkey, and the danger was over. But it certainly concentrated the minds of millions when they realised how near to Armageddon the world had come.

At the time, during the Cold War, those wanting to get rid of nuclear weapons looked altogether far more rational than naïve. In reality, abolishing a weapon that could not be 'uninvented' was impossible. As the great British socialist leader Aneurin Bevan put it, a Britain without nuclear weapons would be like going naked into the conference chamber in negotiating peace with the Russians. But the daily existential horror of annihilation concentrated the minds of ordinary people wonderfully, and from 1957 onwards one of the most powerful grassroots protest movements against the policies of all the NATO governments, especially that of Britain, was the Campaign for Nuclear Disarmament, or CND.

The CND started with unusual leadership – an Anglican clergyman, John Collins, alongside one of the world's leading atheists, the philosopher Bertrand Russell. (Russell would leave in 1960 in favour of a group called the Committee of One Hundred, that believed in more direct action and tougher tactics than the more peace-orientated CND.) Britain had not only many American nuclear bases on its soil – of which more soon – but also the Atomic Weapons Establishment at Aldermaston, whose task was the improvement of the national nuclear arsenal. Soon marches began to take place with thousands of CND protesters walking from Aldermaston to London (or occasionally vice versa), with people of all ages united behind the slogan of 'Ban the Bomb'. Most of these were educated middle class people, many with ties to the arts and media, but there were some trade unionists and thus protesters came from a wide variety of backgrounds.

The close escape from a real nuclear war during the Cuban Missile Crisis of October 1962 convinced many people that being *that* near to annihilation was the best possible reason to get rid of nuclear weapons altogether. The crisis certainly proved a major recruiting tool for CND. It could also be said that the fact that *both* the USA and USSR possessed nuclear arsenals actually prevented war from happening. This latter view was that of the governments of NATO countries in the West. So on the one hand the CND argument convinced many, and on the other the need to defend ourselves by using such weapons as a deterrent equally persuaded others.

Many take the story of CND back up again in the 1980s. Observing university students during the late 1970s and early 1980s would certainly confirm this. The Soviet invasion of Afghanistan in late 1979 scared many, as it clearly marked a new phase in the Cold War. Then the election of Ronald Reagan in 1980 in the USA, a man convinced that such a war could be won, and that the USSR was an 'evil empire', clarified the thinking of many on both sides of the Atlantic. On his side many were filled with a new sense of hope, national pride and patriotism. On the other side people were equally scared witless that World War III might now be conceivable and that millions of British and West Europeans would be the first to die in a nuclear exchange. (The fact that he produced such diametrically opposed responses is in itself fascinating but not something that we can discuss here.)

The Soviet bloc introduced a very dangerous mobile nuclear missile, the SS-20. The USA and its NATO allies responded with similar weapons, the best known being the USA's Pershing and the more generally deployed cruise missile. Many feared that the escalation could provoke a nuclear conflict. Since MAD would destroy the world, this possible apocalypse caused many to listen to CND, with not a few doing so for the first time. By the early 1980s up to a quarter of a million people in the United Kingdom, for example, attended CND rallies and protests, with the Green Party in Germany benefitting politically from the new climate of fear created in Europe's front line state against the Warsaw Pact, the Soviet equivalent of NATO.

In Britain, in particular, the numerous American bases that had existed since the Second World War now became the focus of much protest, since several of them were known to possess nuclear weapons. One of these was Greenham Common, the USAF base in Berkshire, the same county as Windsor Castle. In the case of Greenham, what made the protests special is that they deliberately consisted of women, with some from Wales beginning the demonstrations in 1981. Over 30,000 from all over the United Kingdom set up a Women's Peace Camp there in December 1982. Those who stayed long term became affectionately known as the 'Greenham Women' and their camp entered the national consciousness, even including those who disagreed with their cause or premises. Although the missiles themselves left the base in 1991, the women stayed on some years extra. Their tenacity and good nature impressed many.

But by then the peak of anti-nuclear activism in Britain had passed. In 1980 a former member of CND, the writer and thinker Michael Foot, became leader of the Labour Party. Uniquely in British politics, for his three years in that position the party became the only major British-wide political group officially to espouse nuclear disarmament. In 1983, however, the Labour Party was massacred at the General Election, with its CND-orientated stance being one of the prime reasons for its defeat. The Party's new leadership, while originally pro-CND, soon moderated their stand so that thereafter the Labour Party, along with the Conservative government, supported the alliance with the USA and the nuclear deterrent.

And significantly, in the talks that Ronald Reagan held with Soviet leader Mikhail Gorbachev in the Icelandic capital, the Reykjavík Summit, in October 1986, led in 1987 to a major treaty on nuclear weapons between the USA and the USSR. This understanding in and of itself helped to reduce Cold War tension and make the world a safer place. Then in 1989 the Berlin Wall fell and in 1991 the USSR itself dissolved and the existential threat of nuclear annihilation came to an end.

The world still has nuclear weapons and probably too many of them. But today the real threat is war between neighbouring nuclear powers such as India and Pakistan. The nightmare of Soviet tanks racing to the Atlantic and thereby triggering Armageddon is in the past. We still live in a seriously dangerous world, with the threat of terror bringing death to our own streets. Russia is not exactly a friendly nation. But the Cold War in the old sense of the term is over. Did nuclear weapons prevent it from becoming an exceedingly hot World War III? That is what some believe, while others would be more sympathetic to the approach of CND and would aim to rid the world of such devices altogether. Time and distance will prove who is right.

MARTIN LUTHER KING
AND CIVIL RIGHTS

(1955–1968)

Martin Luther King (1929–1968) was the youngest twentieth-century winner of the Nobel Prize for Peace. Today in the USA his birthday is a national holiday. Around the world he is revered as an apostle of non-violent protest whose courageous stand against racial injustice remains a model to us all. And with the riots in parts of Missouri in 2014, we realise that his dream of harmony between the races, those of European and those of African descent, is one that has tragically still not been fully fulfilled.

He was born in Atlanta, Georgia, to a Christian family, in an age when many African-Americans had no rights. (It is important not to single out the southern parts of the USA for discrimination – while white supremacy may have been legally entrenched in such parts, everyday prejudice was and perhaps remains widespread across the whole country.) In that region of the USA it was said that Sunday was perhaps the most segregated day of the week. White Americans and African-Americans usually worshipped at quite different churches, in defiance of those books of the New Testament that specifically ban such practice. But the one upside is that this meant that African-Americans could learn leadership skills in their own churches, and this was the case with both Martin Luther King, Jr and his father, King, Sr (who was also a pastor).

King was educated at Morehouse College in Atlanta, the premier college for African-Americans in the nation. It was here that he first felt the call to deal with the injustices faced by his race, and that something could be done about it, rather than simply accepting unfairness with resignation. He then attended a seminary in Pennsylvania, forming his lifelong theological positions, and completed a doctorate at Boston University. These two establishments were racially integrated, itself a rarity for those days. In 1953 he married Coretta Scott, who would carry his flame long after his death, and in 1954 he became Pastor of Dexter Avenue Baptist Church in Montgomery AL.

Alabama was at the heart of the Old South, a pivotal state during the days of the Confederacy and Civil War, and attitudes of many among the white majority had not changed much since then. It was in Montgomery that Rosa Parks, secretary of the local National Association for the Advancement of Colored [sic] People [NAACP] was ordered, on December 1st 1955, to move from an area of a bus reserved for white people to sit with coloured [sic] people at the back. Her refusal ended in her arrest. This case became a cause célèbre, a milestone in the struggle for African-Americans to gain legal equality with white people, and it was a baptism of fire in that town for the new young Baptist minister Martin Luther King.

The Supreme Court of the USA made racial discrimination on buses illegal in 1956, a sign of progress. By this time King realised that he must get involved in the issue himself. While a Baptist, he decided to adopt the non-violence principles of Gandhi, deeming them the outworking of the Christian principles that one can read in the New Testament. His true mission had begun.

So in 1957 he was elected as the first ever president of a new body, the Southern Christian Leadership Conference (SCLC). This role propelled him into national prominence, and in 1960 he moved to Atlanta GA, in order to lead the SCLC better and to co-pastor Ebenezer Baptist Church there, with his father.

King's was initially a softly-softly approach. But in 1960 students began a series of lunchtime sit-ins, led by the Student Nonviolent Coordinating Committee (SNCC). Gandhi's principles were very much to the fore with King and many others involved in civil rights, though there were always some who wanted more aggressive tactics. King was arrested at an SNCC meeting, and was fortunate to be released – through the good offices of the Democratic candidate for the Presidency that year, John F. Kennedy.

Kennedy's election in November 1960 certainly helped the cause. But arguably it was the eager advocacy of civil rights by the President's brother, Bobby Kennedy, who was US Attorney General, and that of the Vice-President Lyndon Baines Johnson, a southerner himself, from Texas, that gave King and the activists the help they needed at a national level.

In January 1963 came perhaps the biggest civil rights protests so far, in Birmingham, Alabama. The SCLC organised massive boycotts of shops, sit-ins, staged marches and more besides. They were helped, President Kennedy joked, by the extremist nature of the white response, especially those responsible for public safety. The state's governor, George Wallace, an old school southern Democrat filled with prejudice, also shocked mainstream Americans outside of the region. His famous declaration upon becoming governor of Alabama in 1963 rang out a warning throughout the nation:

> In the name of the greatest people that have ever trod this earth, I draw the line in the dust and toss the gauntlet before the feet of tyranny, and I say segregation now, segregation tomorrow, segregation forever!

On April 12th Martin Luther King was arrested, and on the 16th he composed a letter from prison from his Alabama jail cell. This epistle became nationally famous, as he argued that civil disobedience – the non-violent breaking of laws – was entirely justified if the laws that were being enforced were unjust.

By now King had become the iconic leading figure for the civil rights protests. On August 28th 1963 he and supporters of all races gathered together at the Lincoln Memorial in Washington DC. Many had been part of the March on Washington, and some quarter of a million were present for his speech. His 'I have a dream' oration is now reckoned to be one of the best-known and most revered speeches in human history. Here is an extract:

> *I say to you today, my friends, so even though we face the difficulties of today and tomorrow, I still have a dream. It is a dream deeply rooted in the American dream.*

I have a dream that one day this nation will rise up and live out the true meaning of its creed: 'We hold these truths to be self-evident; that all men are created equal.'

I have a dream that one day on the red hills of Georgia the sons of former slaves and the sons of former slave owners will be able to sit down together at the table of brotherhood.

I have a dream that one day even the state of Mississippi, a state sweltering with the heat of injustice, sweltering with the heat of oppression, will be transformed into an oasis of freedom and justice.

I have a dream that my four little children will one day live in a nation where they will not be judged by the colour of their skin but by the content of their character.

Not surprisingly this speech transformed the situation. Civil rights legislation began to be introduced into Congress, with Lyndon Johnson doing everything to make sure that it passed. King became the 1963 *Time* magazine Man of the Year and in 1964, for his loyalty to the theme of non-violence, he was awarded the Nobel Prize for Peace.

This did, however, not make him popular among whites of a racist nature. As one of his biographers, Clayborne Carson, has pointed out, one of these was the legendary Director of the FBI, J. Edgar Hoover. The FBI now followed King closely, and perceived him as a threat.

Much of the concentration of civil rights now turned to voting rights. In theory, African-Americans had the right to vote, but many states found ways around this and prevented them from exercising their franchise. (Sadly this still happens, albeit on a lesser scale, so the issue remains to this day.) Alabama in particular held out against granting votes and there were ugly confrontations in Selma in 1965. The events there were turned into a film in 2015.

Non-violence is something that we take for granted in discussing King. But what does it involve? It is perhaps above all a way of life – peace brings not just results but shows up the violence of the opposition, the oppressors, as being immoral as well as incorrect. Peace in the face of coercion gives the moral high ground to the protestors. It is easy to throw bricks or 'Molotov cocktails', but that puts the perpetrators in the same category as their enemies and gives ammunition to those who would condemn demonstrators for being no different than those suppressing them. Few people have used peaceful Gandhi-like action as effectively as King.

By this time King realised that there was much racial injustice in northern states as well. In 1966 he realised how much prejudice stemmed from the grinding poverty suffered by many African-Americans in Chicago. But his attempts there were sadly not so successful and the campaigns have been deemed by many to be failures.

In addition, many African-Americans were adopting the more aggressive tactics of new leaders, such as Malcolm X. When X was assassinated in February 1965 he became the martyr for those wanting an emphatically non-Gandhian approach, and the riots that took place in many American cities over the next few years showed that to a new generation of African-Americans, King's inherent non-violence did not go far enough. Furthermore, the attention of radical white youth, especially students, was shifting to protests against the war in Vietnam (a conflict that King also opposed).

King realised that the continuing poverty of so much of the African-American community across the country was at the heart of the issue – it was not just because they were denied political rights or racial equality, but because they were *poor*. This became the new focus of his efforts and such concerns took him to Memphis, Tennessee, in late March 1968, where he helped to lead a march by sanitation workers. Sadly many of the local African-Americans used this as an excuse for rioting and looting, all directly contrary to the principles of non-violence. Then on April 4th 1968 a white racist segregationist, James Earl Ray, spotted King on the balcony of a local hotel, and assassinated him. One of the greatest of twentieth-century Americans was gunned down at a critical point in the history of civil rights.

In 1986 his birthday became an official national holiday in the USA, and in November 2008 Americans elected their first ever president of African ancestry, the Chicago-based Barack Obama. King is now revered worldwide, but while African-Americans have legal rights that were unthinkable when he was born, the USA still has racial tensions to this day. King's struggle continues.

ANTI-APARTHEID AND STOPPING
THE TOURS

(1959)

For just over thirty years any student with compassion for the underprivileged and who had a social conscience gave at least some kind of obeisance to the Anti-Apartheid Movement (AAM), the protest group that did its best to put pressure on the South African whites-only regime to abolish apartheid, or at least to lessen its horrors. And this was not just among those on the political left – many on the right or of no fixed political abode also supported the general principles that the AAM embodied. Most of us were never activists, but happy to sign petitions, grant expressions of goodwill and try, if possible, not to use goods manufactured in South Africa.

The encouraging thing about the movement was that it ended happily, with the dismemberment of apartheid in South

Africa, without the civil war and bloodshed that so many feared. Furthermore, the global iconic figure of Nelson Mandela turned out to be even more heroic and worthy of praise as a moral giant and reconciler far greater than any of us had dared to hope. In so few cases do things turn out as well as the struggle over decades to end racial oppression and segregation in South Africa. Yet with anti-apartheid this has proved to be true.

The origins of anti-apartheid go back to the 1950s, with the goal of spreading an economic boycott of South African goods. In the 1940s South Africa had been far from racially integrated, but the pro-British politics of leaders as revered as Jan Smuts had disguised the reality of the oppression already under way. Under the more overtly white racist nationalist Afrikaner governments that took over, the true nature of racism and brutality became more obvious. Also the harshness of 'separate development' for those of European (mainly Dutch) descent on the one hand and of African descent on the other became legally further entrenched. However South Africa's economy depended very strongly on the ability to export to the West, in particular its precious minerals such as gold and diamonds, and in its economic banking links to Britain, through Barclays Bank. (Ironically this was a bank first formed by many Quaker families, who would have been morally appalled by apartheid.) This left the regime somewhat exposed to Western pressure, and it was in 1959 in the United Kingdom that a group of activists, disgusted by the racist oppression now so blatant in South Africa, tried to see if an economic boycott campaign could work.

So that is how what started primarily as a pressure group began.

But on March 21st 1960, South African police murdered around 69 protesters in the township of Sharpeville – swiftly condemned around the world as the 'Sharpeville Massacre'. The cause was the refusal of indigenous South Africans to carry their pass books. These were internal passports limiting movement from designated segregated areas and restricting jobs. International outrage was considerable, and the levels of disgust at such action rose steadily. So that year the original economic boycott movement morphed, in England and then elsewhere, into the Anti-Apartheid Movement, which it then remained until the end of the nationalist regime in South Africa in 1994.

Much comment on the AAM concentrates on the governmental level. The British government did not always support sanctions against South Africa and those that did not feel as they did. That is certainly important, but it overlooks the AAM as a grassroots movement, some of whose leaders, like the subsequent Cabinet minister Peter Hain, were scarcely adults when their protests led both to success and to global notoriety as well.

Up until 1960, South Africa, as a former British colony, was a part of the Commonwealth. But by that time many of the Commonwealth member states were either large, powerful and non-European, such as India, or nations of white descent that felt that in a multiracial organisation of the kind into which the Commonwealth was now forming, racist South African membership was no longer appropriate. So in 1961 the country was expelled, and not allowed to return until Nelson Mandela was released and in power in the 1990s. That was a victory for the anti-apartheid cause, as was the expulsion of South Africa from the Olympic Games in 1964, for similar reasons.

The British government had recognised, as Conservative Prime Minister Harold Macmillan had phrased it, that the 'winds of change' were moving across Africa and that the time to end colonial rule was at hand. Under Macmillan many African states gained their independence. But from 1965 (under Harold Wilson) to 1980 (under Margaret Thatcher) the British also had the problem of the rogue and European racist state of Rhodesia. It declared independence unlawfully in 1965, and was able to survive in no small way thanks to the aid given it by the South African regime, who enabled the rebels to evade British economic sanctions. Here there was to be a sad ending, as independence soon gave way to the dictatorship of Robert Mugabe, who rules what is now Zimbabwe to this day.

This also led British governments to be dubious about the efficacy of sanctions against the main South African apartheid regime – effective boycotting of all trade and other economic ties against that country were at the heart of anti-apartheid. The majority of Commonwealth members, now including many African countries as well as India, kept up the pressure on Britain to have a more aggressive sanctions policy, and Commonwealth heads of government meetings would often be quite heated as a result. But British of all political persuasions were never fully convinced that sanctions and boycotts would work, and they were also concerned that such action would hurt ordinary South African workers, the vast majority of whom were, of course, African rather than European.

In Britain, therefore, and in other parts of the Commonwealth such as Australia, the anti-apartheid grassroots groups came up with other plans to isolate South Africa in a way that would hit the Caucasian/European ruling elite. They soon discovered that sport was a major way in which to do this. The Europe-originated were sporting fanatics, especially in rugby, and the Springboks were not only among the best in the world but they were also exclusively white European.

In cricket, the regime had already earned international opprobrium by banning the mixed-race player Basil D'Oliveira from world-class play. But it was rugby that was to prove the real Achilles heel. In 1969–1970 young British activists, including the future politician Peter Hain, then a nineteen-year-old student, organised massive protests against the Springbok tour of Britain. While not preventing the tour from happening, so disruptive did Hain and the AAM demonstrators prove to be, that the succeeding *cricket* tour of Britain had to be cancelled. Then, in 1971, like-minded AAM activists in Australia were able to achieve something similar, by so inconveniencing the rugby tour of their country that the follow-up cricket tour had to be cancelled as well.

In the overall scheme of things a cancelled sporting tour did not amount to much, but it did show that grassroots opinion was strongly opposed to the introduction of racist apartheid policies into games such as rugby and cricket. However grand the white Afrikaner minority might reckon itself to be, the outside world thought differently and isolated them very effectively on something about which they cared emotionally.

In the end it was the realisation from within by the Nationalist leadership, especially F. W. de Klerk, that South Africa would *have* to change, that began to crumble the edifice from within. To countless millions of others around the world Nelson Mandela, the imprisoned leader of the African National Congress (the ANC), was both an icon and an enigma as he had not been seen for decades, so long had he been incarcerated.

But when he was released in 1990 it soon became apparent, both inside and outside South Africa, that he was a man of global stature, capable of negotiating the transition from apartheid to majority rule in the peaceful way that most people dreamt of. By 1994 he was president of a free and democratic country, the father of his people, and, as suggested earlier, an icon who truly was worthy of the status that world opinion had cast upon him. There was no bloodbath, no civil war, no mass murder, but an essentially calm transfer of power. The apartheid regime was over.

So while disrupting rugby tours and cancelling cricket matches may not have been instrumental in changing South Africa peacefully – it took the unique genius of Mandela to do that – it had certainly helped and kept the flame alive. Decades of protest resulted in a happy ending.

THE GREENSBORO SODA FOUNTAIN SIT-IN

(1960)

From small acorns do great oak trees grow . . .

Protest movements have sometimes begun small, and with people of whom no one has ever heard. We have all heard of the courageous Rosa Parks, who deliberately sat in the Caucasian/white part of a bus, and showed how segregation on public transport was now immoral and unacceptable. (We see her in the entry on Martin Luther King and civil rights.) But how many have heard of the brave four young African-Americans who deliberately sat one day in 1960 at a soda fountain bar at a Woolworth's in the southern state of North Carolina, and thereby struck a blow for civil rights and the equality of all people?

Thankfully the American historical magazine produced by the Smithsonian Museum *has* remembered them:

On February 1, 1960, four young African-American men, freshmen at the Agricultural and Technical College of North Carolina, entered the Greensboro Woolworth's and sat down on stools that had, until that moment, been occupied exclusively by white customers. The four – Franklin McCain, Ezell Blair Jr, Joseph McNeil and David Richmond – asked to be served, and were refused. But they did not get up and leave. Indeed, they launched a protest that lasted six months and helped change the USA. A section of that historic counter is now held by the National Museum of American History, where the Chairman of the Division of Politics and Reform, Harry Rubenstein, calls it 'a significant part of a larger collection about participation in our political system'. The story behind it is central to the epic struggle of the civil rights movement. (*The Smithsonian*, February 2010)

By February 4th they and their friends had managed to occupy sixty-three out of the total of sixty-six seats available at the soda store (the remaining three being reserved for the waitresses). The key thing is that all of the protesters behaved politely and in a civilised way, keeping resolutely to the non-violent stance of the wider Civil Rights Movement growing up under the more famous leadership of Martin Luther King.

By this time, too, the Woolworth's management had become seriously embarrassed by their peaceful protest – and by the bad publicity and loss of income that the young men were causing the chain nationally.

So the store simply abolished segregation! From then on, anyone could get soda from the Woolworth's bar regardless of race. This marked a major triumph for civil rights, by four brave young men who have mainly been forgotten by history – until the *Smithsonian* resurrected their deeds – but who, in their own small way, truly made a difference.

CÉSAR CHÁVEZ AND THE GRAPES OF WRATH

(1962)

The Grapes of Wrath is a John Steinbeck novel set in the western USA during the Great Depression of the 1930s. But the title could equally apply to the lifelong campaigns of Mexican-American César Chávez, the trade union activist for the poor and oppressed grape pickers in California, who fought for their interests for over forty years.

In Britain we have all heard of Martin Luther King, the great apostle of Gandhian non-violence and civil rights. But in the USA César Chávez, who lived 1927–1993, is also revered for his non-violent, peaceful means of protecting and encouraging the lives of exploited, usually Hispanic, agricultural labourers. His methods were the same as those of King and Gandhi, and show that such irenic means of protest can bring beneficial results.

He was born in poverty, and began life as a child agricultural worker, often missing school because of the need to sustain life. Most labourers were essentially nomadic between different farms, the food harvested dependent upon the time of year. Nothing was ever certain and no work was guaranteed. After service in the American navy during the Second World War, he returned to this itinerant life. But now he was a husband, with a total of eight children to feed by the 1950s.

Some rudimentary form of trade union rights existed, in the form of the Community Service Organisation (CSO) in southern California. One of their most significant young recruits was an initially reluctant César Chávez, who started off as a simple volunteer. He became full time and eventually the director of CSO in 1958. But the CSO was concerned with many issues, including voter registration and protection against the often brutal (and European-ancestered) local police. Chávez wanted more to help agricultural labourers of the kind he had been, so in 1962, along with other fellow Hispanics, he established the Farm Workers Association.

Other ethnic groups were equally exploited, including the many Filipino labourers of the Agricultural Workers Organising Committee. In 1965 this union asked Chávez to help them in the strike against poor pay and bad working conditions in the Delano grape harvest area of California. In 1966 the two unions combined, to form what would eventually become the United Farm Workers (UFW).

Initially power was on the side of the grape farmers. So, adopting the tactics employed by Gandhi in India and later by King in the USA, the UFW decided on a campaign of boycotts, hunger strikes, large-scale protest marches and peaceful picketing. The embarrassment of having so many workers on strike and the damage that this inflicted on their brands soon convinced the owners that they should come to equitable terms with Chávez and his workers. In 1970 they surrendered to the UFW and negotiated a fair and historic series of grape contracts with the workers.

However, grapes were not the only harvest! There were also major lettuce strikes and boycotts after 1970. In 1973 this turned to rioting, which did not chime with the non-violent protest that Chávez employed. By 1974, following the election of a more sympathetic governor of California, the Agricultural Labor [sic] Relations Board was established. This led to state involvement in collective bargaining for the first time, something that was normal in countries like Britain but a wholly new precedent in the USA.

Unfortunately for Chávez, the workers themselves were not united behind him and his efforts. The often notorious Teamsters Union, much older and with greater political clout, entered the fray with its own ends and means, and in 1980 the election of Ronald Reagan as governor meant that the UFW no longer had a friend in high office. This discouraged the grape pickers and other farm workers, so that while the UFW had over 100,000 members at its peak, by the mid nineties this had plummeted to a mere 15,000 or so. The glory years of Chávez appeared to be in the past.

But as his biographer Margaret Rose has pointed out, when he died on April 23rd 1993, tens of thousands of young Hispanic labourers suddenly realised that they had lost a hero. Over

50,000 attended his funeral and today he is, if anything, even more revered than in his own lifetime. By the time of Clinton's presidency he was a figure of respect for white *Anglos* as well as the people from whom he had come.

THE ANTI-VIETNAM WAR MOVEMENT

(1964)

Hey, hey, LBJ
How many kids will you kill today?

The United States, the great superpower, the country that in 1945 beat the combined might of both Nazi Germany and imperial Japan, lost the Vietnam War, against a guerrilla army and the forces of a far smaller Asiatic state. How was this? Was it simply poor tactics or a lack of strategic understanding? Or was it the fact that millions of Americans opposed a war in which their own country was engaged against a power that many did not see as an enemy? This was the antithesis of World War II, in which there were clear aggressors: the Third Reich and the Japanese Empire. How much does the Home Front matter?

And did the protests, along with the hippies and the counterculture of the 1960s, create the 'Culture Wars' within the USA that still make all the political difference in how Americans vote decades after these events? Obviously there are plenty of other factors to consider when we look at such matters in our own day, such as Richard Nixon exploiting the fears of voters of European descent in the South or disquiet among people of faith about abortion.

But the cultural divide between 'red state' and 'blue state' USA, and the fact that so many working-class Americans vote Republican on cultural or 'values' grounds, while astonishing East Coast and West Coast liberals, can be said in large part to stem back to the strong working-class, blue-collar reaction of millions of people against the anti-Vietnam War protesters and the counterculture of which they were a part.

To many of us, the USA never had a realistic chance of winning a guerrilla war in South-East Asia – we should not forget that Vietnam spilt over into Laos and Cambodia as well. But many Americans see it differently, a national humiliation made possible by left-wing, un-American, privileged university kids chanting unpatriotic slogans on the campuses. The Vietnam War is decades over, but the effects of how it played at home in the USA are very much with us still. And that is why the protests are so important, as their implications live on.

Those who have read Graham Greene's famous novel, *The Quiet American* (or seen either of the two film versions), will know that the Vietnam War was a legacy of the Second World War. During the Japanese occupation of Indo-China, down to 1945, the USA actively supported anyone fighting the common enemy. So Ho Chi Minh, the leader of the Communist guerrilla forces, received active aid from the USA.

But in 1945, after VJ Day, the French wanted all their colonies back, from Algeria to Vietnam. They installed a puppet regime that fooled no one, and at the battle of Dien Bien Phu in 1954 the French colonial army was overwhelmingly defeated. That year, in an international agreement that included both the USA and the Chinese, the original country was divided in two – a Communist north, under Ho, and a supposedly democratic republic in the south. As Greene readers will recall, the initial American involvement in Vietnam was in clandestine support of the French. But when France had to depart, American action became more overt, with so-called 'military advisers' from the USA giving direct aid to the beleaguered south.

All this was on the basis of an academic idea – the Domino Theory – that if one state in South-East Asia fell to Communism, eventually all of them would, from Vietnam through to Thailand. As with similar theories about the Middle East in 2003, and Iraq in particular, what works in a university seminar does not always succeed in the real world.

So by the early 1960s, thousands of American troops were serving in Vietnam, and overtly, as it became more and more necessary to increase American strength. This would serve to combat the ever more successful Communist guerrillas in the south, allied to their North-Vietnamese supporters fighting a slightly more conventional war in other parts of the country.

One important thing to remember is the fact that while Britain abolished 'National Service' – compulsory military enlistment – in the 1950s, many other NATO countries, including the USA, did not. So with the war in Vietnam escalating in the early 1960s, thousands of teenage Americans found themselves liable for 'the draft' in the army, navy, air force or the marine corps. Get a low draft number or allocation and a conscript could end up with going to face death in Vietnam rather than two quiet years in a nice army base in Germany or Japan. However, a place at university could result in a deferment, and possibly a less risky officer's posting on graduation. This in itself did not endear students to the working-class kids who had no such options and who often formed the basis of the fighting forces in Vietnam itself.

So the fact that the protests began at places such as the University of California at Berkeley in late 1964, a place both linked with the hippie counterculture and with middle-class privilege, did not endear the protesters to many blue-collar Americans. Many of the protesting students were also on the political left, such as the Students for a Democratic Society (SDS). Tom Hayden (who later married Jane Fonda, herself an anti-war activist), among others, created the SDS. This countercultural movement had a major 'teach-in' at the University of Michigan in early 1965, and the anti-war movement soon spread like wildfire across the campuses of the USA. At the University of California, students began to protest by burning their draft cards, and also burnt President Johnson in effigy. Destroying a draft card was illegal and by the autumn of 1965 the police started to arrest students who did so. But despite the fact that it was university students often doing the protesting, two million of them had managed to achieve deferments by the end of 1965.

In 1966 the legendary boxer, Muhammad Ali (originally Cassius Clay) showed that it was not just students who opposed the war. He refused to go to Vietnam, and was promptly jailed in 1967, until the Supreme Court agreed to his release. Thousands of others who did not want to go were not so lucky. Many had to flee to Canada, and not everyone was able to prove genuine conscientious objection to the war, although some were fortunate enough to succeed.

Anti-Vietnam war riots and demonstrations were not confined to the USA, since many in other countries felt a sense of strong solidarity with the protesters. The 'Grosvenor Square Riots' – a major demonstration in London outside the American Embassy there – took place in July 1967, with many activists arrested. But while the war became a cause célèbre in the UK and elsewhere, Britain refused to take part, to the profound annoyance of President Johnson. (Australia *did* take part, however, with thousands of Australian troops serving in Vietnam.)

By late 1967 the protests were gaining in anger and in size. In October, thousands of draft cards were burnt. Over 100,000 demonstrated at the Lincoln Memorial in Washington DC. By this time the police had begun to arrest many of the protesters, one of whom was the famous paediatrician and author Benjamin Spock, who was apprehended in New York in December 1967, along with over 500 others.

1968 was, as we shall see elsewhere, a year of worldwide student protest, not just about Vietnam. But it was also the year of the Tet Offensive, a highly successful guerrilla action by the Vietcong that caused a major military setback for the American forces. The Americans were trying to fight an underground and elusive foe by traditional means, something that the asymmetric tactics of the Vietcong made increasingly impossible. Whether or not President Johnson would have withdrawn from the 1968 presidential election without the humiliation of the Tet

Offensive is a moot point, as is the extent to which his decision was influenced by the increasing fervour of the anti-war protests at home. But to oppose the war was now becoming mainstream opinion on the politically progressive side of the divide in the USA.

Senator Bobby Kennedy's assassination was a tragedy from many points of view, but while 'counterfactual' history is fun, though unreliable, his death possibly ended the life of someone who could have won the Democratic nomination, won the presidency and then taken the USA out of Vietnam. And there would then have been no Nixon, no Watergate and perhaps no Republican domination of American politics for decades to come.

As a result of this tragedy the Democratic nominee was Hubert Horatio Humphrey, Johnson's Vice-President — we shall look at the 1968 Democratic convention in the entry on Yippies and Chicago. But the turmoil that the protesters caused so worried the average American voter that Richard Nixon, in real life, did win in 1968, albeit with a small margin. The coming to power of a Republican administration in 1969 changed the dynamics of protest, since they represented what Nixon called the 'silent majority' of those who took a very different view of life from that of the average university campus-based protester. And also in 1969 the anti-war SDS split, weakening the wider movement. Numerous major protests took place — with huge rallies in Washington DC and Boston in the autumn. But by 1970 the 'silent majority' became vocal, with *pro*-war rallies now taking place as well.

Then on May 4th 1970 came the 'Kent State Massacre' in

which overzealous Ohio National Guard soldiers shot and killed four unarmed student protesters at Kent State University, injuring nine others. Whether or not students at other universities were pro- or anti-war, this was regarded by millions of them as murder, and there were massive demonstrations all over the country. Over 100,000 people demonstrated against the killings in a rally in Washington DC.

But Nixon had judged the national mood correctly and in a poll taken shortly after the deaths, no fewer than 58% of Americans sided with the National Guard rather than with the students. Middle America had spoken.

Many Vietnam War veterans were anti-war, one of them being John Kerry, who testified to Congress in April 1971. (This would be very costly to him politically in 2004, when he stood for president and Republicans used his return of all his medals against him.) Wider protests continued, with over 150,000 marching that month in San Francisco.

But ironically, Nixon, while utterly against the protesters and their views and lifestyles, was by now doing far more to take the USA out of the war than the Democrats who had taken the country into it. He and his National Security Adviser Henry Kissinger had long been in clandestine talks with the Communist regime in Hanoi and in January 1973 a Peace Accord was signed in Paris. While there was still an American presence in South Vietnam, in Saigon, until the fall of that regime in 1975, for all intents and purposes the Vietnam War was over, certainly so far as the USA was concerned. No more young Americans would be sent abroad to fight and die in the jungles of South-East Asia. In 1975 the Communists won, and the deaths of thousands of American conscripts were effectively in vain.

As argued earlier, it would surely have been militarily impossible for the USA to win, especially as the regime that they were defending in the south was hardly democratic and frequently corrupt and oppressive. And it was a *Republican* president who ended the war, and, in his visit to China, made peace between the USA and the Communist regime in Beijing. But many Americans felt that the humiliation was not inevitable and had been caused not by military failure but by the demonstrations at home.

This feeling, present under Nixon, grew stronger, especially after the election of Ronald Reagan in 1980. The anti-war protests, the counterculture and the whole way of thought in the 1960s became unpatriotic for millions of Americans, who proceeded to vote accordingly.

So the protesters might have won – the USA withdrew from Vietnam. But in another, politically and culturally important sense, they lost, with results that are with us today.

WOMEN'S LIBERATION

(1967)

During the writing of this book hundreds of completely innocent Nigerian schoolgirls were kidnapped by an extremist group, Boko Haram. This group rejects all forms of equality for the female gender, and has probably taken the girls into physical and sexual slavery. Furthermore, a British quality newspaper had as one of its headlines that up to a half of all teenage girls are pressured and coerced into performing acts with which they feel uncomfortable or disgusted.

So are twenty-first-century women free? How historic is Women's Lib, as it is often nicknamed? Has the struggle been won even in the most progressive of developed countries? How many teenager girls have to starve almost to anorexic proportions to be thought socially acceptable to their same-age peer group?

Perhaps oppression continues, but in a different guise.

In many historical accounts, women's liberation began in Chicago in 1967, when a group of women who were all out to help on civil rights discovered that they were still being patronised by the men at the conference. In practice, though, some kind of struggle for the equal rights of women long predates the 1960s, even though the movement as it now exists almost certainly did emerge from the sixties counterculture in the USA and Britain. As we saw in the entry on suffragettes, women have been advocating greater rights for their gender for centuries – from the famous 'Blue Stocking' intellectuals in the eighteenth century, to the pioneers of education for women in school and university in the nineteenth, to the campaigners for equal suffrage in the early twentieth. In many ways what has been happening since the 1960s has been the same basic cause, but put forward in new ways over differing issues.

Women have often been suppressed by men throughout history and stereotyped by looks and employment opportunities. Intelligent women, contrary to cultural and media attempts to portray them otherwise, do not conform to a stereotypical appearance. Women are not confined by nature to particular types of job: homemaker, secretary, teacher, nurse, dinner lady or housekeeper. Nor is size a marker of personal worth or beauty.

On many issues we have come full circle. In 1978 the feminist writer Susie Orbach published her most influential book *Fat is a Feminist Issue*, which sought very effectively to deal with the crucial issue of body weight and self-esteem among women of all ages. At the time it was liberating for many who wished to escape not just from male chauvinist stereotyping, but also from pressure from other women to conform to societal norms in the West. But today, for example, the daughters and granddaughters of its original readers find themselves compelled to fight the same issues all over again, with peer pressure if anything being far greater now than back at that time.

Are women paid equally? In theory this is the case, and sometimes this is even enshrined in law, but in practice, as we all know, the notion of equal pay for equal work remains as elusive as ever, with all kinds of ways around the law dreamt up by those determined that a woman deserves less remuneration than a man. In Britain we celebrate the brave working-class women in Dagenham who fought to achieve pay parity with men, but in practice most Western countries remain as unequal as ever.

Globally, women are very far from equal. We often refer to extremist groups as having a 'medieval' view of the world. But in many such countries today no woman is as influential as, say, the great Abbess Hildegard of Bingen was able to be as far back as the twelfth century, a woman of towering abilities. She wrote to emperors and popes on a level of full intellectual equality. Many nations have still to produce their equivalent of Joan of Arc, a fifteenth-century peasant girl who transformed history in a way that would be utterly unthinkable in many countries of the twenty-first century.

We might all enjoy modern technology but there are still nations in which it is illegal for a woman to drive a car or even to leave the house without a male chaperone and the permission of a male relative. In several places women who were able to go out in public without their faces being covered, some twenty or so years ago, now live in an environment in which were they to do so now, they could end up being stoned or arrested. One could argue that in parts of our contemporary world the situation is getting worse for women rather than better.

Nonetheless, in most Western countries the *legal* position of women is at least better than it was decades ago. The protests, books such as *The Female Eunuch* (1970) by Germaine Greer and the awareness created by demonstrations all helped to change the general atmosphere, and reduce the flagrancy of the intolerance that all too many women have suffered.

In some countries legislation was passed, back in the 1970s, that *theoretically* gave women the same legal status as men. In Britain the Equal Opportunities Commission was established in 1975, after the Equal Pay Act and the Sex Discrimination Act. While discrimination against women unquestionably still exists, at least it is supposed to be illegal.

In the USA, proponents of equality for women tried to have an Equal Rights Amendment (ERA) to the Constitution passed as long ago as 1923. However, this has proved a long and arduous task, one that remains unfinished. Attempts to jump the first hurdle – the approval of both houses of Congress, took until 1972, when both the House of Representatives and the Senate finally passed the legislation necessary – and fourteen years after President Eisenhower, a Republican, had indicated that the ERA was worthy of becoming law. But then it had to be ratified by a majority of the individual states in the USA, in order to become part of the US Constitution itself. As of writing this has still to happen! In the 1980s many women on the political right started to oppose ratification as being against their view of the value and nature of the family. The result has been that not enough states have passed the necessary approval, and the ERA remains in limbo.

Is it all about legislation, however? What matters also are societal attitudes and this has, if anything, worked against women, even in Western countries, let alone those parts of the world where women are oppressed to this day with the custom of centuries.

For example, one can legitimately ask: has postmodernism helped women? Since many leading postmodernists *are* women it might seem an odd question to ask! However, we now live in a society in which *absolute* standards of behaviour are no longer tolerated. In some ways that is a good thing – class antagonism, for instance, suppressed people purely on the genetic chance of the social class into which they were born. But we now have the strange spectacle whereby, to the horror of many feminists of the old school, *some* women think, for example, that participation in burlesque or striptease can be a woman exercising her free choice. Feminists should not be prudes, the argument goes – and the protest group FEMEN widely uses nudity to make its protests, and to get plenty of newspaper photographs as a result for its activists. Is this the cause for which the feminists of the 1960s and 1970s, let alone the great nineteenth-century pioneers, fought so passionately? One rather thinks not! Women in the 1950s might have felt constricted, but were they that much worse off than teenagers today facing the kind of pressure that no woman ought to tolerate, let alone someone so young?

Properly understood liberation for women should be universal, rather than just the privileged right of those fortunate to have been born in the West. Again this is not always popular in our postmodern era, with every cultural outlook now having the right to full tolerance, even if, for example, female genital mutilation (FGM) is regarded as barbaric in most civilised countries. Are we imposing Western imperialist norms when we try to oppose FGM being inflicted on women from certain minority groups in our countries? Or are we proclaiming the full equality of all women everywhere in protecting young girls from this hideous but historically ancient, and in many places hallowed, practice?

All this too is part of the struggle for women to achieve fair and equal status with men. Bra-burning or simple refusal to wear a bra might today seem eccentric and something embarrassing that your grandmother did. The original burner in England, the Australian literary critic and spokesperson for women's rights, Germaine Greer, started the trend in Britain when she was a student at Cambridge in the early 1960s. In the USA, burning was linked to the Vietnam War protests, since the men who refused to serve burnt their draft cards. Burning a bra was thus a symbol of female resistance.

Such symbolism was very much of its time, arguably part of the irresponsibility of the Swinging Sixties. But the idea that a woman teacher should get the same pay as a male teacher, or that women of South Asian ancestry should have the right to choose to be educated if they so wish are both very current issues and show that the work of the nineteenth-century pioneers is far from finished.

THE YIPPIES AND CHICAGO CITY

(1968)

The year 1968 was one of global protest, as more than one entry in this book will testify. One of the movements to emerge during this time was the Youth International Party, the Yippies. They are dealt with separately here because although they were vigorous in their protests against the Vietnam War, they were more than simply an anti-war movement. They also defy conventional analysis, since one may refer to them not as conventional socialists or Communists but as 'Groucho Marxists'. This description of what was more of an anarchist or prankster group summarises them well. They had no official leader as such but a symbol called Pigasus the Pig.

In reality one of their founders, Abbie Hoffman, had been involved in many a prank and in what have been described as 'libertarian socialist' actions, including some against Wall Street in New York. Another senior activist was Jerry Rubin. They were in many ways a political reflection of the counterculture, believing that as much as possible should be free and for the benefit of everyone. Their flag included a marijuana leaf and as Hoffman proclaimed in 1968, the Yippies believed in 'energy, fun, fierceness!' These were not pranks as we understand them – practical jokes – but politically anarchistic acts designed to provoke and to demonstrate a particular cause.

Their biggest prank became world famous if not infamous – their alternative Festival of Life at the Chicago Democratic Convention in 1968. President Johnson had already declared that he would not be a candidate for the presidency that year. Although most people regarded the person who the Democrats chose as their candidate, Hubert Horatio Humphrey, as a decent and personally honourable man, he was stymied by the fact that he was Johnson's Vice-President and regarded by protesters as sharing Johnson's guilt for the war.

But what no one had taken into account was that the Mayor of Chicago was the notorious Richard Daley, an old-time, hard-line politician for whom even the most innocent of pranks, let alone outright protest, was entirely taboo. The Yippies hoped for a countercultural festival with lots of music, but Daley refused any permission.

So instead of a peaceful love-fest came days of rioting, violence and utter mayhem around the area of the Convention, as the heavily armed local police battled ferociously against the activists. As demonstrators often discover to their cost, as soon as you take to the streets, other elements can take control and turn what is supposed to be a fun event into nasty confrontation and bloodshed. Hoffman and the Yippies wanted to have a festival in the park, but Daley and his police would have none of it and they began to clear the area with some vigour.

Other movements now joined in the general mayhem. Figures for injuries remain controversial as each side doubtless exaggerated for effect the numbers of their own people injured, protestors and police alike. But it is reckoned by some that tear gas affected lots of people and *perhaps* some 500 demonstrators had some kind of minor injury. But the authorities insisted that some 152 police were also injured, so it is hard to tell.

The Yippie movement as a whole survived well into the 1970s. The *Yipster Times* was launched in 1972. Now, however, in a very different climate in the USA, it lingers on, but as a shadow of its former self.

One *New York Times* article in December 1968 shows, however, the *real* impact of the Yippie movement and of the Chicago riots. As it rightly hinted, the night of the biggest riots outside the Democratic Convention was the night that the United States decided to vote for Richard Nixon. We saw in the entry on the anti-Vietnam war protests that Middle America, what Nixon called the 'silent majority', were appalled at the mayhem and anarchism unfolding on their television screens. The pranks of the Yippies shocked ordinary middle-class and 'blue collar' working-class Americans, and that November Nixon won, albeit by a small margin. His victory had multiple causes, but the awakening of the culturally conservative working class, part of the bedrock of Republicanism since that time, was a major reaction to the anarchy that the Yippies and others presented to mainstream voting Americans.

From the Yippies of Chicago in 1968 to the educated and

Western-friendly young Egyptian intellectuals of Tahrir Square in Cairo in 2011, the motto of 'be careful what you wish for' should be engraved upon the consciousness of all protest movements. The Yippies got Nixon, the Tahrir Square activists first got an Islamic Brotherhood president and then a return to a quasi-military regime. Protesting can be fun and exhilarating. But it can also cause the very opposite of your dreams.

STONEWALL TO GAY MARRIAGE

(1969)

The writing of contemporary history, as it is called, is always problematic, since the situation can change between the delivery of the manuscript to a publisher and the time that the book appears on the shelves. We see this in another entry, on the Arab Spring of 2011 and its aftermath, and the same is also true with the evolving situation concerning same-sex marriage rights in the USA (in the country of writing, the United Kingdom, the issue is more settled).

So with that in mind, we can look at the changes from the early 1960s. At that time same-sex acts were criminal and frowned upon by most people. This is a radical contrast with the situation today, in which they are legal in the same way that heterosexual acts have been. Full marriage rights are now accorded as well, as opposed to the previous halfway house of civil partnerships.

Discrimination of all kinds has slowly disappeared as far as legal rights are concerned right across the period of our book, the past hundred plus years. Working-class men in Britain finally got equal voting rights to those financially more fortunate in 1918, and full franchise equality for women was introduced in 1928. Civil rights for people of non-European ancestry, as we see in other entries, took quite some time longer, and in countries such as South Africa not really until the 1990s, with the end of apartheid. Similarly, equal pay for women theoretically became acceptable in the 1960s onwards, though as surveys and statistics demonstrate, that battle is far from won. And in terms of *attitudes* as opposed to the law, then the position is often rather bleak. Full equal rights for whatever reason hitherto denied many groups in society is decidedly a work in progress, not an accomplished fact.

With the same-sex or gay agenda, the situation has always been worse in that the practices of homosexuality (whether by gay or bisexual people) have not just been a subject of prejudice but have also been *illegal*. It has, throughout society, been a disadvantage to be a woman or a person of a minority race or colour, but being in that category has never been a criminal offence. Practising same-sex acts has been against the law until comparatively recent times, and in many countries of the world today, most notably in much of the African continent and in parts of the Muslim world, it remains a criminal offence to this day.

And it should be pointed out that there is often a historical anomaly in that countries that have forbidden male homosexuality, culturally and/or legally, for centuries have often never criminalised female same-sex acts, so that what follows is often prejudice not against all gay people *per se* but against gay *men*, even though, morally speaking, according to the ancient mores of many of the world's religions, there is no distinction between the two.

In the 1950s in the USA, same-sex attraction was regarded as a deviation or indeed mental aberration, a classification that was not withdrawn until the early 1970s. And homosexual acts were strictly illegal. Prosecution both in the USA and the United Kingdom was sporadic, however, and often inconsistent, with entrapment frequently used as the means of catching people and finding them guilty in court. And those with the right social or political connections often escaped punishment so long as a veil of discretion was imposed.

The result was a semi-tolerated and semi-suppressed netherworld, where the authorities would be aware that gay people would frequent particular bars or clubs, but much depended on the attitude of the local police, or, as was notoriously the case of a particular Mafia-linked bar in New York, the Stonewall Inn, a matter of bribing the local police.

Many gay people in Britain and the USA felt that if women could enjoy equal pay, and if people of African or Asian descent could enjoy freedom from discrimination, so too could people of homosexual persuasion. So along with the wider civil rights movement came a new subset, that of Gay Rights.

On June 28th 1969 a riot took place in protest against a police raid on the Stonewall Inn, situated in the trendy, funky part of New York in Greenwich Village. There had been similar riots and protests before, notably in California, but for some reason these particular disturbances became iconic, and have traditionally marked the start of the active part of the Gay Rights Movement. So it is not so much that this was a protest, but that *this* protest, at Stonewall, became the trigger for a whole movement that followed on from those events. Today in Britain the premier rights organisation is Stonewall, founded in 1989, and famous for its links to high-profile media personalities, such as the actor Sir Ian McKellen (Gandalf in six well-known films).

In Britain, homosexuality was decriminalised in the raft of changes in the 1960s that also made abortion legal and divorce easier. For a while in the 1980s, sex education in schools was not allowed to promote same-sex activity as an equal option, but that was repealed. Now, with gay marriage granted full legal equality to its traditional counterpart, gay people enjoy full equal status in the law. With secularisation more the norm in Britain, religious views that might have prevailed up to the 1950s are no longer the norm.

In the USA, the federal structure of the country means that it is often up to individual states to determine what is and is not legal in their particular jurisdiction. Several states have had referenda on issues such as gay marriage or the use of marijuana, and as part of what have been called the 'Culture Wars' in the USA since the 1960s, such votes have frequently been hotly contested, with deep feelings on both sides. Not until very recent times has homosexuality among men been legalised, and not all parts of the USA today recognise gay marriage as being legally equal to the traditional version. So in the USA it is still an issue in progress, with the numbers of people of religious views unhappy with such change being exceptionally high for a Western country.

As for Africa, it is, as we saw earlier, still illegal in much of that continent, It is interesting that Russia, now adopting a far more nationalistic perspective, is now a part of Europe in which gay rights are going backwards rather than forwards. The future of this issue remains uncertain.

WOODSTOCK AND THE
COUNTERCULTURE

(1969)

Countercultural hipsters living on the edge one day, rock and roll multimillionaires the next . . . And in Britain, often knighted by the Queen, or awarded a CBE, the honour that is the next rung below being a knight . . .

The hippies of the counterculture in the 1960s were fashionable rebels against what they regarded as the stifling conventions of safe, middle-class Western society. Coming as many of them did from prosperous homes, it was easy to 'drop out' for a few years, and then re-enter normal life, with a good, well-paid job and, by now, an excellent pension as well, since the 'baby boomers' who made up such a large part of the sixties counterculture are now of retirement age. Of course, not everyone abandoned their ideals, but countless made compromises with the system that they had so opposed in student days, and conformed in deeds even if inward beliefs remained the same. Those of us of a certain age know of what we are speaking, as we have seen it happen time and again to those either of our own generation or (in your author's case) to a generation slightly senior.

This is the context in which it is surely best to look at the counterculture and at one of its most iconic events that took place as the sixties were ending, the Woodstock Festival, otherwise known as a three-day celebration of peace and music, from August 15th–18th 1969. The venue was a farm in the Catskill Mountains of upstate New York.

Most people now know it for the 1970 film, one that had to be given an adult certificate, not because of the music, but as a consequence of filming so many people taking illicit drugs. Rock festivals had been held before, and by 1969 the counterculture was itself no longer new, with the lifestyles that went with it spreading from San Francisco on the Pacific Coast to London thousands of miles away. Thousands already lived in communes or in squats, took what today would be regarded as comparatively mild but still dangerous narcotic drugs, and wore their hair long and frequently unkempt.

Many rock groups of the era had sold millions of copies of their recordings, so the combination of commerce and contemporary music and making serious money were not new phenomena. The fact that rock musicians were supposed to be *against* the culture – hence the description of their movement as a *counter* culture – was gently ignored by everyone: one of the most iconic groups of that time, the Rolling Stones, were to achieve huge financial success when they hired a very respectable and devoutly Roman Catholic prince of Bavarian royal ancestry, Prince Rupert zu Loewenstein, as their business manager. But the zeitgeist was still there, even if alternative fashion shops in London were raking in profits from those wanting to look trendily unfashionable.

Those wanting to put together a festival of countercultural values – what they called 'An Aquarian Exposition' after the sixties idea that we all now lived in the 'Age of Aquarius' – were wholly sincere people. And they clearly had no idea of how incredibly popular and earth-shattering their planned two days (it became three by mistake during the event) would turn out to become. They were sure that 50,000 would attend at the most – still a large number but nothing like the crowds that in fact came. In fact, eight times as many – about 400,000 people – finally turned up, and the governor of New York State, Nelson Rockefeller, had to send in law enforcement, not so much to arrest thousands of drug-takers but to deal with the chaos that had been created by such large and unexpected numbers. Being hippy, though, meant enjoying the mud that sloshed everywhere as a result of the rain, and one of the more surreal moments of the festival was the sight of thousands of participants trying to send thought vibes to the clouds to stop the downpour.

It was almost a case of anyone who really was anybody being a performer at Woodstock, although a lot of the bands both famous then and subsequently were in fact not there. But Jimmy Hendrix, Joan Baez, Ravi Shankar, the Grateful Dead, Janis Joplin, Jefferson Airplane, the Who, Joe Cocker and countless other groups *were* present and added their lustre to the events. Those not at the event – such as the Beatles and Bob

Dylan – were to regret their absence, especially after the film in 1970 made such a global impact.

But overlooked at the time was the fact that the citizens of the local town of Bethel voted against such events ever happening in their neighbourhood again. (Apparently the current inhabitants take a different view.) Nixon had been elected president in November 1968 and taken office in January 1969, and the reaction of mainstream USA was not so friendly towards anti-establishment rock music, mass skinny-dipping, men with long hair and illegal drugs. The festival-goers might have represented the zeitgeist of the 1960s, but already the times were changing and the national mood among ordinary Americans was no longer the same as we saw in the entries on Vietnam and on the Yippies.

So while the media would refer to the 'Woodstock Generation', one could argue that by 1969 their time was passing. There would be other major festivals, such as the one that took place on the Isle of Wight, in Britain, in August 1970, with many of the same artists performing there (like Joan Baez and The Who) as at Woodstock. But the festival at Altamont in the USA in December 1969 – at which the Rolling Stones *did* participate – turned violent, with several deaths. While large-scale rock concerts continued, they would not be quite the same. And when they did happen, such as Live Aid in the 1980s, which took place both in England and in the USA, they were no longer countercultural festivals or celebrations of alternative values and lifestyle. Live Aid was a fundraising event in a good cause, the relief of countless thousands facing death and famine in Africa.

But apart from all that, the major record labels began to realise the vast spending power of the 'Woodstock Generation' and the commercial possibilities of exploiting this for large corporate profits. While some of the performers were to die tragically young – such as Jimi Hendrix – others went on to become centimillionaires, with vast personal fortunes, country houses and lifestyles that would be gently mocked in satirical magazines such as *Private Eye*. The music would continue, and in theory many of the core values of that era, but *in practice* the situation would be totally different from the idealism of their origins.

And thus, to many, the rock stars were no longer truly countercultural, a perception that would play into the hands of Richard Nixon, the Republican candidate for president in 1968, in terms of building up blue-collar resentment against the seeming wealth of those claiming to opt out of society while coming themselves from privileged backgrounds.

Then in 1973 came the great oil price hike, caused by events in the Middle East, with a massive and negative economic impact on the West. Life became more serious, and the national prosperity – which rather ironically the counterculture needed in order to survive – vanished, in fact, never to return. The Woodstock era of countercultural protest against society was over.

So was Woodstock really a *protest*? Was it simply rich kids trying to have fun, as some have suggested? This would explain why 'blue-collar' America reacted so strongly against the counterculture, with political results that are with us still. In today's financially squeezed times, young people work hard, don't do drugs and take life seriously. We live in a truly different world.

GREENPEACE: SAVING THE PLANET?

(1969)

Frankenstein foods? Or food that saves the lives of millions of poor people across the planet?

Greenpeace began in the late sixties/early seventies (people differ on the actual foundation date) in connection with protests against nuclear weapons tests in the Pacific. However, today Greenpeace is active on a much wider realm of issues, so we ought to see the context in which it acts before looking in detail into its more famous campaigns.

Few things arouse more ire today than genetically modified crops – or GM foods, as they are often described. How you see everything is influenced by the answer that you give to the question at the start of this entry. And it may also determine how you see this book! At the time of writing the European

Community's chief scientist resigned over the very contentious issue of GM crops. To her as a scientist – and in her mind, therefore, completely objective – there is no *scientific* problem with GM-grown foods, and so they are an entirely safe product both to manufacture and to eat. But to the Green Party members in the European Parliament the situation is *very* different indeed, with genetically modified anything being both dangerous and therefore unacceptable.

The same kinds of issues arise in many other fields, from abortion (a swift and safe procedure vs. murder) to climate change (a scientific fact that changes how we care for the planet vs. a monstrous lie that deceives us into taking unaffordable and unnecessary actions). Feelings lie deep on both sides, and the issues raised by Greenpeace are at the heart of many of them.

Ironically, when scientists say that global warming is a genuine and man-created phenomenon, many environmental activists believe fully in science! On *this* issue both Greenpeace and the scientists are in full accord, and it is often those on the political Right who would engage in what both the majority of the scientific community and pro-Earth groups such as Greenpeace would insist as 'climate change denial' or a refusal to see the obvious truth of the damage done by toxic emissions to the atmosphere and our health. But on GM crops, for instance, the Green activists (political and issue-based) are on one side, and the political Right *and the scientific community* are on the other. Complicated? I think that the answer to that is yes – and both the political Right *and* Greenpeace are also correct to say that scientists are nowhere near as objective as they like to think of themselves as being. Greenpeace began around 1969–1970 as protests against nuclear weapons testing near Japan. Those born after 1991 (the end of the Cold War) can have little idea of how scary was the threat of mutually assured destruction – total global annihilation in the event of a massive nuclear war between the two superpower blocs of the USSR and USA, and the 'nuclear winter' that could result, an event that would probably have blotted out *all* life on the planet, let alone the human race. (We look at this in the entry on CND.) So Greenpeace at that time was active in wanting to save the planet in more senses than one: not just to preserve the global ecosystems from nuclear contamination – which even the tests could achieve – but humanity as well.

It was for a double purpose that Greenpeace bought one of their most famous symbols, the ship that they renamed *Rainbow Warrior*. It had been a British government vessel, but Greenpeace re-engaged it as a boat that it would use for protests. In 1985 it was for such dual use that they sent it to the southern Pacific, to near New Zealand, with the twin goals of preventing the dumping of nuclear waste (which would have contaminated much of the marine ecosystem) and also saving the local whales, which were in danger of being hunted to extinction. However, the ship was interfering with French nuclear testing, and on July 10th 1985 secret service agents from France sank the ship, in Auckland Harbour, in New Zealand. One of the journalists following the story died in the explosion, and the French government was duly condemned by world opinion.

Other Greenpeace activities, those of the three decades and more since 1985, have been controversial, entirely depending upon your own point of view. For some, Greenpeace is saving the planet, its inhabitants as well as its ecological balance, rainforests, rare plants and animals, and the polar ice caps, the melting of which would cause global catastrophe whichever view of climate change you might take. For others it represents the twenty-first-century equivalent of the Luddites in early nineteenth-century England, who deliberately destroyed industrial machinery to save the jobs of ordinary labourers – but therefore made work far harder for everyone.

One of the areas of controversy, for example, that have been raised on social media was the use of GM crops to help stave off a famine in Zambia, a landlocked country in southern Africa. The Zambian authorities sided with non-governmental groups, such as Greenpeace, to ban the import of GM crops. But others were furious, since they argued that starving people were in desperate need of food from whatever source it came, organic or genetically modified.

Go into a major food/grocery store today and there will be a large amount of *organic* food or milk, a product of the enormous success of organisations such as Greenpeace in changing the minds of ordinary people. Their advocacy and worldwide protests have probably changed your shopping habits whether you consciously choose such products or not. Your power as a consumer affects strongly the way in which large corporations listen to what Greenpeace is saying.

However, the use of vandalism to prevent experimentation in GM crop growing alienates many – who feel that legitimate scientific discovery is being literally destroyed by protesters – while encouraging others in their opposition to 'Frankenstein science'. Again this is a highly contentious issue, with passionate feelings being aroused on both sides.

We are thankfully not anywhere near in danger of nuclear

Armageddon as we were during the Cold War, so the need to prevent the kind of weapons testing prevalent until 1991 is now diminished. But is nuclear power safe? Once again many scientists argue that it is, if anything, the *safest* form of energy – it creates very little contamination to the ozone layer of the atmosphere, for example, as opposed to obvious pollutants such as coal – but others, including Greenpeace, remind us of its dangers, as the recent catastrophe at the Fukushima Daiichi power plant in Japan, which went into meltdown, showed in recent times.

Will the polar ice caps melt? How is 'global warming' caused? Is it human irresponsibility – as, in this case, the majority of scientists in agreement with Greenpeace would argue? Or is it the quirk of history, as a minority of scientists along with people who describe themselves as 'climate change sceptics' would have us believe? One of the reasons why this debate is not arcane are the quite hideous consequences for all of us, let alone future generations, if those arguing for human agency in climate change are correct. For if Greenpeace and the scientists are right, then we can wipe ourselves out every bit as effectively as the threat of nuclear annihilation threatened just a few decades ago. We can boil the earth to extinction . . .

With the stakes this high, it is very easy to understand the emotions involved, and why neutrality is hard to achieve, even for scientists! One comment made by the outgoing Chief Scientist to the EU is interesting, as she suggests that with GM food – against which Greenpeace is zealous – for many people the issue is not so much the food or the science itself, but the fact that some of the world's largest corporations are behind GM and make serious profits from it.

Electorally the 'Greens' may not be *that* large in Britain or the USA (though they are growing all the time in the former), but in much of Europe they are major players and sometimes they are or have been government itself, such as in Germany. Quite often they are politically to the left of many of the older and more traditional parties, and being anti-capitalist is very much part and parcel of such an approach. So the fact that particular multinationals manufacture and sell GM crops, whether to help the starving in the Global South or not, makes their products wrong in and of themselves. This is, of course, to look at the issues *ideologically* rather than *scientifically* and therefore complicates debate between protesters on the one side and scientists on the other – it is not so much, therefore, a dispassionate discussion of *facts* but of *beliefs*.

Greenpeace is thus at the heart of such issues, and it is an example of how simple protest can change government policy, influence millions of consumers and all at grassroots level upwards. Whether or not they are right is for you to decide!

THE MINERS' STRIKES AND THE BATTLE OF ORGREAVE

(1973–1974 and 1984–1985)

We are all grateful today for vacuum cleaners or for our Dyson machines when we clean the house. It is so easy to order books, food and more besides online. But do we think of the fact that in the 1950s the vacuum cleaner made obsolete thousands of domestic service jobs, making generations of servants redundant? For that matter, take the fact that today, with a simple click of our mobile phone, we reduce the need for perhaps millions of shopkeepers? Technology changes things. Life is much easier. But the jobs done by countless generations of skilled labour are now relegated firmly to the past. And in many cases whole communities would be involved around the same factory, the same coal mine or the same trade . . .

Such was the fate of hundreds of thousands of coal miners in

Britain in the 1970s and 1980s. Pit villages in which every male had worked down the mines, hewing coal, for over a hundred years or even longer, suddenly had no purpose. The very core of the community had vanished, along with the pride and powerful sense of identity and shared purpose that went with it. It was not just a case of vanishing jobs. An entire lifestyle and way of existence disappeared with an entire class of worker no longer wanted or needed in a scary new and very unfamiliar modern world.

Many of us travel far, see different places, enjoy friends whose jobs or lives adapt well to change, and live in heterogeneous environments in which the very diversity of our surroundings makes life so interesting.

But imagine being raised in a community in which every man did the same job, as their fathers, grandfathers and great-grandfathers had done before them, where diversity was unknown and in which a trip even to the nearest town seemed a huge distance to travel. The modern world would seem a very frightening and threatening place.

For some of us technical change is a cause for celebration. This chapter, instead of having to be posted, with a walk to the post office (another vanishing public place) and money spent on stamps, can now be sent both free and instantaneously to the publisher. Galley proofs and putting in changes by hand are now all things of the past. Life is much easier. And, of course, we are now all encouraged to be environmentally conscious. Coal is a notorious creator of carbon emissions, and is one of the worst pollutants imaginable. Britain has often been careful in the past with preventing such pollution, but places such as Poland or parts of West Virginia in the USA have seen environmental devastation in the recent past caused entirely by coal mining. China, once a chief polluter, has begun to clean up its environment.

But what if you are from a pit village in which it was all right to leave school at sixteen with limited qualifications because you knew that you had a job that you thought was for life, just as generations of your male ancestors had done before you? And now the mine was closing, and all the solidarity of social life around the pit and its workers was being grassed over, and the new (and foreign-owned) utility company needed smart young people with university degrees to do a job that replaced yours with technology that you do not understand?

All that would be rather scary, would it not?

The miners' strikes of the 1970s and 1980s might seem rather a long time ago. But in fact they have repercussions that are very much present with us still, long since the coal mines that have been closed and grassed over made this an issue of history.

So we can look at the events themselves and then examine the profound results they have for us in the twenty-first century. They embody the transition between the old pre-technology, class-based world of the past and the global, high-technology and often atomised era in which most of us live today.

In the strike of 1973–1974 the miners had the upper hand. In late 1973 the nations of the international oil cartel OPEC drastically increased their prices, so alternative forms of energy also saw a dramatic rise. The price of coal was now much higher, and very importantly the stock of coal held by the government declined greatly as the result of the strike by the miners. In those days coal was a nationalised industry, and nearly all the pits were in the hands of the National Coal Board. Not only that but much of the country's electricity supply was coal-generated, soon with dire consequences.

As a result, the government faced an acute energy crisis. The prime minister and the Cabinet therefore put Britain onto what was nicknamed the 'Three Day Week', with businesses only able to use electricity for three days per week. Domestic consumption was also reduced. Then in January, when 81% of the members of the National Union of Mineworkers (NUM) voted to strike, having rejected an inflation-busting 16.5% wage increase, the issue became political. The government decided, as part of its overall strategy of reducing trades union power, to call a general election on the question 'Who Governs Britain?' The result was one in which the Conservatives won the most votes but the Labour Party the most seats, and so Harold Wilson, the Labour leader, became prime minister. The new government gave an instant 35% wage increase to the miners.

However, in 1978–1979 many in Britain felt that the trade unions were going too far, and in May 1979 Margaret Thatcher won the election and became Conservative prime minister, leading a government well to the right of those of previous Conservative regimes. She was determined to beat the miners, and made sure that if a strike ever happened, the government would have large reserves of coal, much of it bought from overseas. Many power stations were switched to non-coal sources of energy, reducing considerably the national dependence upon coal. In 1983 she won a second general election, with a larger majority, and was more determined to implement effective curtailing of trades union power than ever.

So on March 6th 1984, when the government announced

the intention to close twenty pits as no longer viable, battle was joined. The reason that the National Coal Board and the government gave was principally economic. These pits were simply uneconomic to maintain, and they could only continue at a loss. This was a rational decision based upon cost, but that is not how the miners saw it. The pits were, for their communities, not simply a place where you worked but a way of living, a cultural rather than economic issue.

One key factor was that the president of the NUM, Arthur Scargill, was a left-wing socialist, and so saw the strike in the same political terms as the government. And he played straight into the hands of the prime minister when he ordered the NUM to strike *without a legal strike ballot*. This meant that striking miners could not claim welfare benefits and would inevitably get into financial difficulties the longer the unofficial strike continued.

Not only were the NUM on strike, but they also engaged in what it called 'picketing' or action to prevent material from getting through. In the South Yorkshire district of Orgreave, the picketing escalated into violence. Thousands of picketers had come from across Britain in solidarity with the miners, so there were a good 5,000–6,000 activists present. And the police too, also in their thousands, had constables and officers from around the country. The confrontation became highly aggressive, especially when mounted police started to charge the protesters, and many were injured. Since the events were deeply controversial it is hard to know precise statistics, but 95 picketers were charged with rioting, 51 of them were injured along with 72 policemen. It soon entered local legend as the 'Battle of Orgreave'.

But since the government had prepared ahead for all

contingencies, they were able to retain the upper hand. In addition, non-militant miners in some areas rejected the tactics of the NUM and formed a new group, the Union of Democratic Mine Workers. Many of these miners went back to work, and the class solidarity of the NUM, going back to the 1880s, was dissolved. Slowly but surely many NUM miners also decided that enough was enough and voted to go back to work, though with those in Yorkshire and Kent wanting to hold out.

The strike ended on March 3rd 1985, with a victory for the government. As a result they were to end up being able to close far more than twenty pits. The Labour Party was divided, with its leader Neil Kinnock having asked for an *official* strike ballot at the beginning of the action, something that would have made all the difference had it happened.

Today the coal mining industry is privatised and scarcely exists. A whole way of life has come to an end. And Margaret Thatcher was able to use her defeat of the miners in 1985 to help the Conservatives to win the general election in 1987. The strike swiftly became part of folklore, with the reactions of people in Britain very much divided between those favouring the miners and those against. The famous film *Billy Elliot* was centred around the activities in the ancient coal mining areas of Easington and Seaham, and the subsequent musical has kept the story alive.

For many people, a large number of whom will recall the events of this chapter, the issue was about progress, about catching up with technological change, about enabling customers to have safer, environmentally immensely cleaner, and financially much cheaper fuel, to run the home or up-to-date factory or office. And for most of us reading this, all that is true as well. Not only that, but when we change jobs we do not have a lifestyle change as well; our means of earning a living might be different but we live in the same place, have friends who also work in similar ways – some of them, perhaps, telecommuting and able to do their jobs at home – and nothing *fundamentally* alters.

For tens of thousands of people in radically different jobs – coal miners, steelworkers, shop assistants – the situation is altogether different. Whole communities, as we just saw, revolve around just one skill. Close that and the whole reason for existence of the town or village changes forever.

The coal strikes in the 1970s and 1980s in Britain were about pay and working conditions. But they were also about tradition, culture, communal solidarity, lifestyle and centuries of living in the same place, living the same lives as the coal miners' ancestors had done for centuries. The strikes were also, more controversially, about politics – who controlled the country, about the relationship between government and trade unions, and who would win in a confrontation between the two sources of power. In other words, much of it was a proxy battle, in which actual coal mining was a side issue.

The clashes, which in the 1980s were sometimes to become quite violent, were thus not merely *industrial* but also *cultural* and also highly *politicised*. And they were about *change* and how traditional jobs survive in one of the most rapidly technologically transforming ages in our history. It was, one could argue, about *identity* as well as about how much a miner should be paid and the safety of the conditions in which he worked. (And always *he* – this was a job for men, in an era in which the disadvantages faced for centuries by women were rapidly disappearing in a much more gender-egalitarian new era.)

This is the essential background to looking at the miners and their strikes in the 1970s and 1980s. They were doing more than defending their jobs: they were sticking up for whole communal lifestyles, centuries of solidarity and class loyalties. And the other side was defending *its* values as well – the modern world, cheaper and safer fuel, being part of a world economy and protecting the environment for future generations.

With the politics of the strikes often becoming toxic and very unpleasant, very powerfully dividing national opinion, we forget the cultural issues that were, in many ways, like the elephant in the room. The political and social effects have lasted often decades after the original clashes were over.

Today, in many parts of the Western world, low-skilled white men feel a deep sense of alienation to the new global high-technology era in which we live. Such groups feel disenfranchised and are the easy prey for extreme-right groups who share their distaste for the modern age. In Britain, many such people are former miners, who lost the battles of the strikes, and their children, who with no mines in which to work, are alienated from the twenty-first century. Like their counterparts in Europe and other parts of the world, they are part of the trend towards polarised and atomised politics, with all the dangerous consequences with which we now live.

THE NESTLÉ BOYCOTT AND BEYOND

(1977)

How much do we think about what we eat or drink? And do we determine our purchases by brand preference or by reviewing the ethics and marketing practices of the company? Most of us buy what we prefer to use based on price or taste, but shopping is – or certainly *ought* to be – more nuanced and complex than that. For the fact is that we do not buy particular brands and foods in isolation, and the context in which we eat or drink anything can change.

Rowntree, a company known mainly for their chocolate products but also for famous UK brands such as Fruit Gums, was started and owned by a Quaker family of profound social conscience and deep moral probity. They built a special social housing village for their employees, who were treated far better than ordinary workers at other companies. Much of the profit

144 | Christopher Catherwood

went not to enrich the family but into social foundations, many of which still exist, to foster the good of everyone.

But then in 1988 Nestlé, the big Swiss conglomerate, also famous for its chocolate, but notorious for its milk products, bought Rowntree, one of the world's most ethical companies. And it is the milk products that have caused many people to urge fellow consumers to boycott Nestlé and all its extensive holdings. The protests against that company first began in July 1977. Now, around forty years on, that boycott still exists, with campaigners using their friendship circles and today social media to urge people never to buy a Nestlé product. The company defends itself: 'Nestlé UK & Ireland is a subsidiary of Nestlé SA, the world's leading nutrition, health and wellness company.' They say:

At Nestlé we use four simple words to describe what we offer: 'Good Food Good Life'. We believe that having a healthy, balanced approach to the things you eat and drink helps you to enjoy life. Nutrition is just one aspect of 'Good Food Good Life'. Great taste, consistent levels of quality and safety, value for money and convenience also enhance our enjoyment of food and ultimately life.

In essence the argument against Nestlé involves the selling of powdered baby formula and other baby foods to developing countries in breach of international marketing standards. Millions of women in Africa, Asia and Latin America have been convinced either not to breastfeed their newly born babies, or to augment their breastfeeding with Nestlé milk products and baby foods instead. To Nestlé, this is normal, modern, practical sense, and their milk is a product like any other. Those opposing the company do so because millions of babies become sick or die as a result of the unsafe water with which the formula is mixed. Baby Milk Action posted this statement:

> UPDATED Nestlé formula labels poster: Nestlé claims to believe breastfeeding is the best start in life for a child, but promotes its infant formula around the world with claims such as it '*protects*' babies and is the '*gentle start*'.

But the company fails to state that the formula is not sterile and so by the time the child develops health problems owing to unsanitary conditions, either the mother's milk has dried up or the baby is too ill to survive. Take this quotation from one of the organisations that opposes Nestlé, Breast Milk Action:

The World Health Organisation says:

> Globally, breastfeeding has the potential to prevent about 800,000 deaths among children under five each year if all children 0–23 months were optimally breastfed.

That is 11.6% of all deaths amongst children under five years old could be prevented by breastfeeding. Expensive baby foods can also increase family poverty. Poverty is a major cause of malnutrition. Nestlé have agreed to drop their further claim to provide a 'natural start' by mid 2015 because of the constant pressure exerted by the boycott. However, they will not drop the other claims.

So buying Fruit Gums in 1987 helped the poor and starving,

and in 1989 exactly the same product went into the corporate profits of a multinational that has been accused since the 1970s of exploiting exactly the same category of people. One day eating fruit pastels is an act of virtue, and on another it is, depending of course on your point of view, one of vice.

There are many boycotts of various goods or countries taking place all the time. The Nestlé instance is a symbol of wider expressions of consumer power, of the ordinary 'little person' being able to do something effective against global giants. One person alone can do nothing, but millions worldwide can move mountains! But the Nestlé example also shows that however hard people of conscience might try, if the average person in the street continues to think as an isolated consumer – 'I buy what I like and forget about the context' – then the corporate interests will continue unabated.

In 1984 the United States was persuaded – after much debate – to drop the boycott since the World Health Organisation of the United Nations declared itself happy with Nestlé's compliance with the very strict code on how such products ought to be sold. However, in Britain many remained unconvinced of this and in 1988 they began a new boycott that is still in operation.

Nestlé naturally insisted on its innocence!

Many developing countries didn't fully implement the Code. So, in 1982, we became the first manufacturer to introduce our own policy, drawn from the WHO Code, to regulate how we marketed breast milk substitutes in developing countries. We refined this policy in 1984, after consultations with stakeholders including the WHO, the United Nations Children's Fund (UNICEF) and civil society organisations.

Nestlé today, decades after 1977, remains one of the strongest multinational companies around, and is still unapologetic. Who is right? Even if the boycott has not succeeded altogether, a major multinational had to take significant notice of a global boycott against its products. And since all brands live or die by popular perception, and boycotts have adverse effects on even the most powerful of consumer brands, Nestlé had to act.

Today some people in the UK, for example, boycott Starbucks, the coffee chain, because it uses foreign subsidiaries to lessen its tax exposure. For those of us who prefer other brands of coffee this is not a problem – and likewise your author never eats Fruit Gums – but for others, to stay away from their favourite cafe is a hardship. To all boycotts there is a cost, and if the cause is right, it is surely worth paying.

THE DIRTY MOVEMENT AND HUNGER STRIKES

(1978 and 1981)

Hunger strikes – the refusal to eat food – have been at the core of many of the protest movements that we look at in this book. The early suffragettes, for example, used hunger strikes to embarrass the Liberal government of their day. Gandhi frequently fasted in prison and also out of it, as did César Chávez, the Hispanic trade union rights activist. And around the world, long periods of fasting have been seen by many religions as being meritorious, a way of concentrating upon God and of ridding one's mind of spiritually unimportant necessities.

But all these are associated in some way or another with *non-violence*, although the suffragettes were, as we saw, not averse to throwing bricks through windows or other semi-violent forms of protest.

However, some of the most infamous hunger strikes have been those perpetrated by men who had in some form or another been associated with considerable violence, and in particular with nationalist terrorism. Governments are always loath to concede *political* rights to prisoners, and it was to gain such special treatment status that many a suffragette went on hunger strike before the First World War, as did Gandhi during the long struggle for Indian independence.

The same was true of the prisoners of the Irish Republican Army, the IRA. Today the IRA, and its political wing, Sinn Fein, is a party of government itself, holding several posts in the Northern Irish Cabinet, including that of Deputy First Minister. While there are disturbances from time to time, and the occasional riot (as much Protestant, one should add, as Nationalist or Republican), by and large in our time the province is thankfully essentially at peace.

But back in the 1970s and 1980s this was very far from being the case. And again one should say that there was terrorism on both sides, with the hard men both Protestant and Catholic alike being locked up by the British, often in the same prison but very carefully separated into different wings so that the terrorists of each side would not meet those from the other.

In the late 1970s the IRA demanded to be given political prisoner status, just as the suffragettes had before them, and with a similar response from the British government then as earlier. They resented being treated as ordinary prisoners or simply as criminals. Furthermore, in the case of the IRA they did not recognise British rule in the province as being legitimate, so did not think that their jailors had the right to treat them according to what the IRA regarded as foreign law.

In addition, since many of those in poverty in both Catholic and Protestant communities were scared of the terrorists, whether IRA or Loyalist, it was difficult to get evidence that would stand up in court, since witnesses were terrified of testifying. So many IRA prisoners were incarcerated without trial, understandable in the circumstances, but looking like political imprisonment to many outside the United Kingdom, especially to IRA sympathisers in the USA.

Their initial protests were in the form of non-cooperation. They also had what were euphemistically called 'dirty protests', refusing to remove excrement from their cells. But with the coming to power of a much tougher British prime minister in 1979, Margaret Thatcher, it became clear to the IRA that they would have to adopt more drastic tactics, since she was firm in her opposition to give any credence to their requests.

This, therefore, involved a hunger strike in which an IRA prisoner was prepared to go all the way and to die if necessary. One such man appeared: Bobby Sands. From a part of Belfast (Rathcoole), he had been radicalised at an early age through mistreatment by local Protestants, and had joined the Provisional IRA as a teenager. In 1977 he was involved in a gun battle with the Royal Ulster Constabulary and was imprisoned. So in 1981 he was ready. And unfortunately for the British there was a vacancy in the House of Commons in the parliamentary seat of Fermanagh and South Tyrone. This was a district that if the Catholics fielded a single candidate they could capture from the Unionists. Sands, now on active hunger strike in prison, became the 'Anti-H Block' candidate – the H blocks being the prison wings where both Protestant and Catholic terrorists were imprisoned. In April 1981 he won the by-election, so technically became an MP. This gave him an even higher profile still, so when he died of starvation on May 5th 1981 he became a martyr to the Republican cause, an overnight hero to many a young Catholic radical.

As many as nine IRA prisoners died after him, starving themselves to death in prison. None of them quite achieved his iconic status. It was certainly a blow for the British authorities. But the Catholic Church was also unhappy with the deaths and pressure was put on the major Sinn Fein leader Gerry Adams to call off the hunger strikes. Eventually this happened and the era of such drastic action ended.

Mrs Thatcher never saw the hunger strikes as a legitimate means of protest, and when she survived an attempt by the IRA to blow her up, along with most of her government, her resolve if anything strengthened. But in 1985 she undertook direct talks with the Irish government that infuriated not the Catholics but the Protestants. And behind-the-scenes talks between the British and IRA *did* take place, which in 1998 resulted in the Good Friday Agreement. This ended nearly thirty years of carnage in Northern Ireland, a peace process that, while tenuous, still holds together by a thread today.

THE OLYMPIC BOYCOTTS

(1980 and 1984)

How political should sport be? Can we differentiate completely between playing a sport and the country in which the sport is being played?

In the 1980s this became a major issue beyond the original controversial boycotts and protests in cricket (which we look at in the entry on the anti-apartheid movement). For at the end of 1979 the Soviet Union invaded Afghanistan in order to rescue a pro-Moscow regime there that might otherwise have been overthrown.

In itself the issue of Afghanistan – a war that the USSR was to go on to lose – became one of the cause célèbres of the Cold War. It is now mainly known for the fact that the massive arsenal of weapons that the USA gave to the Islamic guerrilla forces fighting the Soviet occupiers were later used by many of those same rebels to fight against Western interests when the Taliban took power – a phenomenon known as '*blowback*'. Even today, Afghanistan, now infamous as the base of Al-Qaeda's war against the West in 2001, continues to be a nation at war.

The then president of the USA, Jimmy Carter, felt profoundly deceived by the behaviour of the Soviets, with whom he had been engaged in peace talks aimed at lowering the frighteningly high numbers of nuclear missiles held by both camps in the Cold War. With the invasion of Afghanistan, most countries realised that the USSR had taken a step to escalate international tension to dangerous levels, and overnight the world seemed to have become a much more unsafe place.

But what had all this to do with sport? Why should athletes, swimmers, horse riders and gymnasts care about international policy? The answer is that the venue for the 1980 Olympic Games was Moscow, the Soviet capital. This had been arranged years before, in an era in which détente between the pro-Soviet East and pro-American West was supposed to be working. But suddenly, with the USSR a pariah state and countries around the world in political uproar – fully including the world's biggest Communist country, the People's Republic of China – the venue of the 1980 Games was a major problem.

For the American government under Jimmy Carter the answer was simple – all states should boycott the Moscow Olympics. Memories were strong of the Olympic Games in Berlin in 1936, and the argument worked both ways on that consideration: on the one hand countries should not have enabled Hitler to have a propaganda coup in hosting the event, but on the other he and his racial policies were humiliated when the African-American Jesse Owens triumphed over Aryan German athletes at the Games themselves. But for 1980 the Carter view prevailed in the USA – no American competitor should attend and legitimise Moscow by taking part.

For many Western allies that argument held with them as well. For example, West Germany, long the powerhouse of European competitive strength, boycotted the Games completely. So too did China, no democracy but a nation that had reconciled itself to the USA during Nixon's presidency in the 1970s. Many countries across Latin America also boycotted Moscow, as did many nations in Africa in the British Commonwealth, such as Kenya, whose long-distance athletes had long been among the best in the world.

Some nations left it up to their own Olympic Associations to decide. In Britain Mrs Thatcher, the new prime minister, was naturally fully in favour of a boycott. But the British Olympic Committee split according to disciplines: the gold medal-winning equestrian team decided to obey the boycott, as did the yachters, but most sports, most notably athletics, decided to go and participate. The United Kingdom was therefore split.

So in 1980 some of the world's top athletic nations, such as the USA, West Germany, China and Kenya, were absent, and Britain was there in part but not in whole. Needless to say, countries that had hitherto not won so many medals, because of strong American or West German strength in previous Games, now performed winning races or events, and the Soviet bloc countries, most notably of course the USSR itself, gained far more medals than ever before.

Soviet foreign policy was not altered one iota by the 1980 boycott, but it did make clear to the USSR that military adventures did have consequences. In the end the Red Army had to withdraw ignominiously and defeated from Afghanistan, an event not caused by the sporting boycott but all part and parcel of the eventual fall of the Soviet bloc between 1989 and 1991.

The 1984 Olympics had been pre-preplanned for Los Angeles. This time the Americans had committed no heinous acts worthy of a boycott, at least so far as most of the world was concerned. But the 1980 boycott had stung the USSR, and so they took revenge in 1984 by boycotting the Los Angeles Games, and persuading nations sympathetic to them to do likewise. However, two Communist countries in Europe – Yugoslavia (a neutral country in Cold War terms) and Romania, a hard-line totalitarian state but which cleaved its own path, did turn up in Los Angeles in 1984, as did the People's Republic of China. Nowhere near as many states boycotted these Games as the fifty-nine who absented themselves from Moscow in 1980.

Thankfully for the Olympics, and for the cause of sport in general, the choice of Seoul, the capital of South Korea, proved uncontroversial in 1988. The Olympic Games were no longer politically toxic or exploited for Cold War rivalry. And by 1992, when the Games took place in Europe, in Barcelona, the Cold War was over.

Not everyone has been happy at the way in which host countries use the Olympic Games for blowing their own trumpets. Some were queasy about the Games taking place in Beijing in 2008, since China, while unquestionably one of the greatest sporting nations on the planet, is not exactly a pluralist democracy with human rights either. The same applied to the Sochi Winter Olympics in Russia in 2014. Nonetheless, the protests and controversies of the past do seem to be over so far as sport is concerned, and that, we can all hope, is for the better.

SOLIDARITY AND THE PATH TO FREEDOM

(1980)

How many electricians have changed the world, and won a Nobel Prize for Peace in the process? For just that was the happy outcome for Lech Wałęsa, a shipyard electrician from the port city of Gdańsk, on the Baltic coast of Poland. From small things – a local strike – can protests grow, in this case into the overthrow of Communism and a nation restored to freedom after decades of foreign oppression and mass murder.

In the seventeenth and eighteenth centuries, as we shall see again in looking at the protest movements in the Ukraine, Poland was an integral part of one of the biggest and most powerful countries in Europe. Large swathes of what are now part of the Ukraine, Russia, Lithuania and Belarus were parts of this great nation. Then, in the later part of the eighteenth century, internal weaknesses led to the vast Polish–Lithuanian Commonwealth being unjustly carved up between Prussia (the state at the core of the future German empire), Austria and Russia. No Poland existed again until 1918, when the defeat of the Central Powers and the intervention in European affairs of the then American president, Woodrow Wilson, led to the recreation of that once mighty country yet again. But Danzig, the major Polish port, remained a German city under League of Nations protection. It was not until the disintegration of the Third Reich in 1945 that Danzig finally became Gdańsk, Poland's major outlet onto the Baltic Sea.

But liberation from the Nazis was not the end of the story for millions of Poles. We forget that while Britain went to war for Poland in September 1939 the same month saw one of the most cynical agreements in history, the Nazi–Soviet Pact, between Hitler's Third Reich and Stalin's Soviet Union. Poland was carved in two, much of its territory stolen for ever, and millions of Poles massacred not just by the Germans but by the Russians as well – with thousands of innocent people massacred by the NKVD (the notorious KGB's predecessor in terror) at Katyn, Poles slaughtered by *Russians*. Liberation from Germany in 1945 did not mean freedom, but many decades to come of oppressive Soviet rule over a once free and proud Polish people.

This is the essential background to the extraordinary events of 1980–1989, in which a few brave Poles, the shipyard worker Lech Wałęsa among them, were able to effect a genuine liberation of their country, and miraculously without bloodshed. We remember the Nobel Peace Prizes of people such as Martin Luther King or Nelson Mandela – as we should – but forget the equally heroic efforts of Wałęsa.

We also tend to think of trade unions as being on the political left, which is what they are in many countries. But what if the government itself is Communist and is the universal employer? Unions under such authorities tended to be mere stooges for the dominant party authorities, and not at all, as they are supposed to be, working in the actual interests of the workers themselves.

Poland from 1945–1989 was such a country. But some protesters and activists wanted genuinely to defend the rights and livelihood of ordinary working people. Wałęsa, in the now Polish city of Gdasńk, was among them. As early as 1970 he was already protesting on behalf of the shipyard workers about price rises and labour conditions. By December that year there were major strikes in Gdańsk and neighbouring cities, which by early 1971 were becoming too successful for the Communist authorities, who sent in thousands of police and special armed forces. As with all such events in authoritarian countries it is hard to gauge precisely what happened next, but some estimate that as many as 45 workers were killed by government forces and hundreds injured. The so-called People's Republic of Poland was killing its own citizens. But the strikes cost the job of the Polish Communist leader, Gomułka, who had to resign because of his failure to keep the nation under proper control. At least, though, the Soviets did not invade, as they had done in Hungary in 1956 and in Czechoslovakia in 1968.

Wałęsa was lucky to be alive, and in 1976 he was sacked for his illegal trade union activities. This did not deter him however, nor did being arrested on several occasions by the Secret Police. He was supported by some courageous outsiders, who had established the Worker's Defence Committee (KOR in Polish) for this purpose.

And on August 14th 1980, as writer and witness Timothy Garton Ash described at the time, when a strike broke out at the Lenin Shipyards in Gdańsk, Wałęsa vaulted over the protective fence that prevented unauthorised people from entering the shipyard and changed history. (He had been forbidden access by the authorities so his leap was technically trespassing.) To rewrite a famous phrase from the moon landings, a small leap for one man proved eventually to be a giant leap for the freedom and eventual liberty of millions of men and women in Poland.

Various clandestine trade union organisations had existed already. But what changed things in 1980 was the establishment of the first truly free and non-government national trade union, *Solidarność*, or in English, the Solidarity Free Trade Union. Starting in Gdańsk, Solidarity spread like wildfire across the whole country, with at its peak, before the crushing of dissent, some *ten million* or so members, around a third of the active working age population of Poland. The workers in a supposed workers' state were organising their own trade union, and Lech Wałęsa became chairman of their organising committee and then president of the new union in 1981.

Totalitarian states do not love independent-minded groups that they cannot control. Much controversy has occurred over whether or not the Polish Communist authorities wanted the Soviets to sort the problem out by staging an invasion, or whether or not they always wanted to carry out the suppression themselves. Either way, on December 13th 1981 General Jaruzelski took the latter option and declared martial law in Poland. Solidarity was made illegal, Wałęsa and other leaders were arrested, and some innocent people died.

Very much in the tradition of Gandhi and of Martin Luther King, the Solidarity activists had decided to adopt the policy of non-violence. There were no bloodthirsty riots of the kind that would have justified even worse state action. Wałęsa was finally freed in 1982, permitted to return to work, although only in his original role as an electrician, but the world estimated him differently, awarding him the Nobel Prize for Peace for that year. Martial law was formally lifted in 1983, but in practice the oppression continued. However, the Solidarity trade unionists and sympathetic activists did not give up and in 1986 some of them were amnestied.

However, as other chapters in our book show, 1989 was a major turning point in Central Europe, with several Communist regimes crumbling peacefully from within, such as in Hungary, or with not inconsiderable violence, as in Romania. In Poland the wave of strikes from 1988 onwards convinced the increasingly shaky Communist authorities that a deal had to be reached with Solidarity. 'Round table' discussions began, with Wałęsa leading for his side. Solidarity was finally recognised as a legitimate trade union, and a political deal was also hatched. This latter part of the deal was not so favourable to democracy, however, since the Communists still insisted on no less than 65% of the seats in the Polish Parliament (the *Sejm*) being reserved for their own members. In the elections that followed, all but one of the free 35% of seats went to Solidarity.

But in the rest of Europe Communist regimes were collapsing like ninepins. In August 1989 Poland had its first non-Communist prime minister, and the following year, in 1990, in genuinely free elections, Wałęsa was elected as the first free democratic president of Poland in many decades.

Today Poland is a full-fledged democracy, a member of the EU and of NATO, and a lynchpin of both groups. The decades of foreign rule and of authoritarian government are finally over. The protest of a few workers in a shipyard had repercussions beyond their wildest dreams and a rare happy ending.

BRAVE NEW PEOPLE AND
PRO-LIFE ACTIVISM

(1984)

In August 1984 the usually sedate and serene annual Christian Booksellers' Convention in the USA was the scene of protests and mayhem. One of the leading Christian publishers in America, InterVarsity Press [*sic*], had published a book that spring entitled *Brave New People*, the author being a New Zealand expert on recent medical ethics and their spiritual implications. The title was deliberately based on the dystopian futuristic novel by Aldous Huxley, *Brave New World*, and was in essence a book examining the dangers of some of the new discoveries in medical technology. What was the harm in that? Well, one enormous problem was the fact that in strictly limited circumstances it allowed for *therapeutic* abortion – in the case of serious health risk or even death to the mother, or in instances such as rape.

Now we come to something that to millions of Americans is *the* key and prime determinant issue of how they vote: abortion. Is abortion a medical procedure like any other? Does a woman have the right to choose whether or not her pregnancy goes to full term? Or is abortion *murder*, plain and simple?

On the answer to that question has hinged the last several American presidential elections, at least so far as millions of Evangelical and Roman Catholic voters are concerned. To them, a candidate's view on abortion is *the* main criterion upon which they vote. The president of the USA appoints the Supreme Court, and as far as *millions* of American voters are concerned, getting a Supreme Court that would overturn the decision that court had made on legalising abortion on January 22nd 1973 in *Roe vs. Wade* is the most important thing that a president can do.

To the secular side in the USA – and the even more substantial secular majority in the United Kingdom – this is completely incomprehensible. Books have been written with titles such as *What's the Matter with Kansas?* that suggest liberal utter bewilderment at the regular, almost clockwork decision of millions of working-class voters in Kansas to vote not for the Democrats but for the party of the rich, the Republicans. But in fact the answer is entirely simple. The 'religious right' in the USA describe themselves as 'values voters' and in voting Republican that is exactly what they are doing.

In Britain, abortion hardly figures on the political radar at all. It is entirely up to individual members of Parliament to vote not on party grounds but completely on their own conscience on whole rafts of moral issues, from gay marriage through to abortion rights. To the astonishment of visiting Americans the

United Kingdom simply does not have the 'culture wars' that have dominated much of the USA's whole political framework for decades, and in particular the matter of abortion since its legalisation by the Supreme Court in early 1973.

As a result, the USA has become highly polarised on what one might call identity issues and on moral disagreements that in Britain hardly rate a mention at general election time. In the Democratic Convention one speaker or another – in the 2004 election it was one of Al Gore's family – gets up and proclaims that Democrats believe in 'a woman's right to choose'. And then the Republican Convention will have speeches announcing the latter party's strong support of what is described as 'family values'. Thus the polarisation of American politics continues, and not on issues of economic policy – though they are of course discussed – but on *morality* and its symbolic representation, abortion.

With the judgement of *Roe vs. Wade* passing into American law, there are now inevitably fewer demonstrations and protests in favour of the pro-choice option. But *pro-life* activism continues all the time, especially now that the Republican Party and the so-called 'religious right' overlap so much, even more so since the rise of the 'Tea Party' grassroots movement on the strongly conservative end of the political spectrum in recent years.

And frequently the feelings on abortion run deep. In the UK the debate is often on timing, and the amount of weeks after which an abortion becomes medically undesirable, especially if there is no health risk to the mother. Thankfully, the advance of medical technology means that danger to the mother – or even death – which was a major problem until comparatively recent times, is increasingly unlikely. But that has meant that abortions late into pregnancy have become morally distasteful, since the mother is not in danger and a foetus is often capable of independent life.

But in the USA much of the pro-life movement takes what one might describe as a very absolutist stand – no abortion at all in any circumstances whatsoever, regardless of rape or of any jeopardy to the mother. If there is a choice between mother and foetus, the foetus or unborn child comes first and if needs be the mother dies. Thankfully that is now medically unlikely, but since for many if not most of the pro-life movement in the USA, abortion is no different from murder, then their absolute criteria remain.

It is important to say that Evangelicals and Roman Catholics disagree on the extent to which civil disobedience is the answer to the widespread use of abortion in their country. In 1991, in Wichita Falls TX, tens of thousands of Christians gathered together to aim to prevent abortion clinics from functioning, a direct action that resulted in many otherwise very law-abiding people being arrested for disturbances, obstruction and other trespasses. Not all Evangelical leaders felt comfortable with this, feeling that it was better to trust to prayer and democracy than to break the law. Nonetheless the protests drew attention to that cause, as was intended. And remember – to pro-life people, since abortion is nothing less than murder, the scale of abortion in the USA is to them no different from the Holocaust of Jews in the 1930s. Theirs is not the majority view in the USA on the subject, but it does explain the depth with which they feel it.

Decades on, the feelings of those on both sides has not abated. With the rise of the 'Tea Party', itself named after the famous eighteenth-century protest, when angry American colonists in Boston emptied British tea into the sea, that same sense of injustice and alienation continues. Perplexing though it may seem to today's secular majorities, religious sentiment has not gone away. It is, of course, strange to British people that the majority of pro-life activists in the USA are also zealous opponents of gun control and supporters of capital punishment, but then many quirks of history in the United Kingdom are equally baffling to Americans. The abortion debate and the 'culture wars' that it helped to spawn are with us still.

THE TWO INTIFADAS

(1987/2000)

Did the Royal Family order the death of Princess Diana? Was the moon never really landed upon by American astronauts? Was 9/11 a wicked Zionist plot? These are all dark-conspiracy theories, in which most of us choose *not* to believe, but which are articles of absolute faith to many, however wacky they may appear to the majority of people.

We, however, live in a Western democracy with plenty of sources of information. Those who have only restricted, censored information know that most of what their government tells them is either a downright lie or a decidedly self-interested version of the truth. Under such regimes, there is not much difference between an official statement and a theory that the moon is made of cheese. For decades, many in the Arab world sincerely believed in the nineteenth-century Tsarist-manufactured conspiracy theory of *The Protocols of the Elders of Zion*. This was a Russian *Ochrana* (state security) invention that said that there was a secret Jewish cabal out to rule the world. In both Nazi Germany and until very recent times indeed, in more than one Arab country, this fraud was actually taught as truth to millions of schoolchildren.

All this is a necessary background to the story of the two Palestinian protests or intifadas against Israel from 1987–1991/3 and 2000–2005. These intifadas led to the killing of hundreds of entirely innocent civilians on both sides, Palestinian and Israeli, and took that beleaguered region no nearer to peace at the end than it had been at the beginning.

To some people this is as much a war as a protest. But there is a good case for saying that while it seems now more like a conflict, it *began* as a protest, and escalated as the fighting worsened. So it is surely legitimate to include it in a work about protests.

The existence of the states of Israel and Palestine raise some of the most profoundly contentious issues on earth, and have done so ever since the division of the region in the 1940s. Objectivity is almost impossible to achieve, so deep and visceral are the feelings on each side. While writing this, your author saw a debate between a British supporter of Palestine and British Zionists (supporters of Israel) in which there was enormous heat and very little light on either side. The very existence of the state of Israel itself is not recognised by many in the debate, and on *both* sides there are those who insist that the actual borders of the respective states are not man-made but decreed by God! Agreement is therefore very hard to achieve, which is perhaps why it has not happened, despite decades of international mediation and effort. The tragic reality is that it probably will never take place at all.

That is a great deal of background for an issue that ostensibly starts in 1987! But in fact we need to understand the beginning point, and the redrawing of the borders in 1948. For it was in this year that Israel was created in the first place, with the areas promised to a Palestinian state being allocated not to a new country, but to Egypt in the 'Gaza Strip' and to Jordan on the 'West Bank'. Then in 1967 Israel seized those same territories in what is now called the Six-Day War.

In 1987 an Israeli army truck ran into and killed four Palestinian civilians. The Israeli authorities said it was a sad accident, the Palestinians said that it was a deliberate act, and the riots began.

This was the 'First Intifada', which while starting in 1987, either ended in 1991 or in 1993, depending on the source that you use. Either way it was an unpleasant escalation of violence between Palestinian youths and Israeli Defence Force (IDF) soldiers. The youths would throw rocks, the IDF would defend itself with rifles, a Palestinian young man would be killed, which meant that more of his friends would hurl rocks, the IDF would again defend itself, more Palestinians would be killed . . . It really was what the cliché says it was: a cycle of violence. And what would always make it worse was the increasing youth of the protesters, with many of them being children. The IDF soldiers tried to break their arms rather than shooting them, but while this meant that far fewer were killed, thousands of children were hospitalised with broken limbs, news which went down very badly on American television when a crew from CBS broadcast such incidents on prime-time news.

By the time of the Madrid Peace Summit in 1991 (which is when some date the end of the First Intifada) well over 1,000 Palestinians had been killed and some 38,000 injured – this alongside 90 Israeli deaths (military and civilian) and some 2,500 injured.

Others date the end of the first wave of protests as being the Oslo Peace Accords of 1993, when, in theory at least, both the leadership of the Palestinians – the Palestinian Liberation Organisation (PLO), under Yasser Arafat, its legendary father figure – and the Israeli government promised to find a peaceful, internationally backed solution to the problem.

However, things were alas not so simple. In *theory* the PLO was prepared to contemplate a 'two-state solution' or an independent Palestinian state living harmoniously alongside the existing Israeli state, and with globally recognised borders between the two entities. But this was betrayal to the new player on the scene, the Islamist organisation, Hamas. In theory it was (and is) quite possible to be a Christian member of the PLO, as that group is a secular *nationalist* body embracing Palestinian Arabs of all religious beliefs and none.

But Hamas is an *Islamic* movement, for Muslims only. And for them, once a territory is under Islamic rule or the *Dar al-Islam*, it is *always* under Muslim jurisdiction. (This was seen in Spain with an act of extremist terrorism – to the perpetrators, Spain was once Muslim *Andalus* and thus eternally Islamic.) For such people the two-state solution that is obvious to many was blasphemous and spiritually impossible. And while the PLO continued to control its old heartland of the West Bank, Hamas increasingly became the movement of choice of the Palestinians living in Gaza, the territory contiguous to Egypt.

Hamas did not believe just in throwing rocks. While the First Intifada ended in 1993 by any reckoning, Hamas now launched suicide bombers against Israel. From 1993–1997 Hamas's thirty-seven suicide bomb attacks in Israel led to nearly 300 Israeli deaths, nearly all the latter being entirely innocent civilian targets.

As the Palestinian joke goes, do you want to get better for free in a Hamas-run hospital or get worse and go bankrupt in one run by the PLO? The PLO regime in the West Bank was accused of all kinds of ineptness, bungling and outright corruption, charges that could not be levelled against the more puritanical Hamas. (The fact that it was the PLO who – theoretically, at least – wanted peace and a two-state solution, and Hamas who wanted to continue fighting, shows the dilemma that many Palestinians faced.)

In 2000 the Israeli politician, the former military commander and national hero, Ariel Sharon, sparked the Second Intifada. Again, was his action – a stroll around the sacred precincts of a part of Jerusalem holy to both Jews and Muslims alike, the Temple Mount or Haram al-Sharif – an innocent act or a massive and deliberate provocation? The answer, as so often, depends entirely on your pre-existing beliefs and outlook.

Whatever his intentions, the fury he provoked among the Palestinian population was massive and the hideous cycle of rock throwing and shooting in return began all over again, and with similar dire outcomes. Within days of the start, on September 26th 2000, some thirteen Palestinian young men lay dead. But this time the Hamas leadership had something far worse than rocks thrown by children to unleash against the IDF. A new wave of suicide bombers was unleashed, with the inevitable large-scale civilian casualties among defenceless Israeli civilians. This in turn escalated the violence further – doubtless as Hamas had hoped – and Sharon now became prime minister and determined upon revenge. The IDF tanks and planes blitzed Hamas-controlled areas, killing not only the military leadership but hundreds of Palestinian civilians as well.

And just to make sure that ordinary Israelis would be safe against suicide bombers the Israeli government now ordered the building of an enormous defensive wall, to keep Palestinians either out altogether or to make entry for them as difficult as possible, so that security police could check everyone for hidden explosives. Just after the demolition of the Iron Curtain in Europe, a new wall filled with symbolism was now constructed to separate Israel and the Palestinian-ruled territories on the other side. In fact, as some realised, Palestinians were also cut off from each other, as the wall blocked old short cuts.

Then, in 2005, Sharon astonished everyone by taking out all the Israeli settlers who lived in Gaza from the region, thereby declaring that any Israeli/Jewish settlement in that region was now over. The Palestinians had long been furious at the stealthy enlargement of Israel by Jewish migrants expanding the areas in which they lived – usually in heavily guarded compounds and the settlers themselves Jewish people who had only recently come to Israel from places such as the USA. Now it was an *Israeli* government taking a peace initiative. Everyone agrees that the Second Intifada ended in 2005.

However, in 2006 Sharon, the former warrior turned

politician, sank into a coma, from which he never recovered, living on unconscious until his death in 2014. Since then the conflict between Israel and the Hamas-controlled Gaza area has, if anything, been far worse, with Hamas firing rockets deliberately into civilian areas of Israel, and IDF counter-attacks once again killing hundreds of innocent civilians as 'collateral damage' for targeting the Hamas leadership. The demonstrators who began by throwing rocks in 1987 started a long period of violence and death from which the region has never recovered, with peace as distant a prospect as ever before.

TIANANMEN SQUARE AND THE
JUNE 4TH INCIDENT

(1989)

As an old Chinese saying goes, 'may you live in interesting times'.

China is one of the oldest *continuous* civilisations on earth, so large and powerful a country that it is in one single nation more united and populous than, say, the countries of the European Union combined. All of the latter have different histories, many with massive breaks in continuity, such as the period we nickname the 'Dark Ages' following the decline and fall of the Roman Empire, the only power to have united all of Europe under a single ruler with one imperial language: Latin. While China has seen occasional eras of confusion, what we see in that country is a nation whose history has continued unbroken for thousands of years. China has a sense of its own importance and destiny as the Middle Kingdom, unmatched anywhere else.

All that is the essential background to the extraordinary events in the capital Beijing between April and June 1989. In the early twenty-first century China is indisputably the number two global power, and in the same way that the twentieth century has been named 'the American century' for the USA, so too might our own times see China become the predominant superpower soon.

(Economists and political commentators disagree on the details or on the extent to which the USA *might* decline. But most experts agree upon China's rise in some form or another, whatever happens in parallel to the USA.)

For China to become a superpower would be a *return*, since up until the rise of European power in the fifteenth and sixteenth centuries, the Chinese Empire was, certainly along with the huge Ottoman Empire, either one of the world's greatest powers or perhaps *the* mightiest, as it had been for centuries past. We often forget this in the West – it is not often that schoolchildren even so much as learn Chinese history let alone know it – but you can be sure that the Chinese of the twenty-first century remember it very well indeed. The era of Western and European hegemony is a comparatively recent development. For decades China's rulers have longed to return to the status quo pre-Europe.

The one thing that stops this from happening is internal chaos. China in the nineteenth century saw just such strife, with rebellions such as that of the Taiping, when an eccentric Chinese rebel claimed to be the younger brother of Christ and organised a mass uprising against the reigning dynasty. Again this rebellion is unknown in the West but nonetheless tens of millions of Chinese civilians lost their lives. The weakening of the final imperial dynasty, that of the semi-foreign Manchus, enabled the West to gain a toehold in China greatly to the latter power's disadvantage. The mayhem that followed the demise of the Manchus and lasted down to the rise of Communist rule in 1949 saw yet more civil war, even more millions killed, a Japanese invasion in which over *twenty million* Chinese were slaughtered and an overall weakening of a once proud empire in the face of the West.

Chaos, in other words, is something that the Chinese elite fears constantly. And during the Great Proletarian Cultural Revolution, Mao Zedong, the paramount Communist leader, inflicted just that on his *own* people. While figures are hard to come by, it is entirely possible that over *40 million* and maybe far more than that perished during 1966–1976. Those of us who know survivors of that terrible time understand full well the hideous psychological scars that mass murder, exile to remote rural areas, persecution and imprisonment inflicted upon the fortunate millions who *did* survive the turmoil and carnage. Among the victims who emerged alive but scarred was a former leading Communist apparatchik Deng Xiaoping, and his son Deng Pufang, who was crippled for life by rampaging Red Guard revolutionaries.

In 1974 the calm and collected Zhou Enlai was able to persuade Mao from purging Deng further, and Deng was allowed back into government. Mao died in 1976 and after a shaky period of transition Deng emerged from the rubble in 1978 as the senior party member and de facto ruler of the country. He was able to hold this position until 1992, but even though he then formally retired, behind the scenes he was still very much one of the most powerful and influential people in China. During his fourteen-year rule he transformed the country. He kept the Communist Party in its position of unique political authority, but allowed very considerable degrees of economic freedom, making the country a far more prosperous place. Unfortunately with such policies, the income discrepancy between ordinary Chinese and the newly prospering middle class grew substantially, as did the corruption that is virtually inherent in a one-party state. And as many grew richer with economic liberty, not a few wondered why political freedom could not be granted as well.

So in 1989, when students began to protest against party tyranny, Deng saw not enthusiastic young people eagerly wanting to spread democracy and freedom but a serious threat to the stability and integrity of China. All he had tried to achieve after the chaos of the Cultural Revolution was, he and the party elders felt, now jeopardised.

So, as in so many entries in this book, once more perception is everything! From the point of view of those of us in the West, the desire of the students coming together in Beijing from April 1989 onwards to have full *political* freedoms – what the USA would call inalienable human rights – was entirely justified, since we have enjoyed them for centuries in our democracies. But to Deng and the elite the abolition of one-party rule could cause chaos, both of the kind seen in 1966–1976 but also from the decline of the Manchu dynasty in the early nineteenth century onwards down to 1949 and the Communist takeover.

Initially the students were concerned about the death of the recently retired Chinese Communist eminence Hu Yaobang. But soon protests in his memory gained a far wider remit, the advent of democracy and Western-style freedom and civil rights in China itself.

What truly sparked the demonstrations on a large scale was an editorial published by the Communist Party on April 26th in the *People's Daily*, the official mouthpiece of the party. This condemned the student sit-in and protests, and raised the spectre of the Cultural Revolution. Already Deng and other hardliners were worried about the potential for chaos.

The editorial, in fact, had the precise opposite effect from the one intended. By now over 100,000 students were semi-permanently in the square. The students had given seven demands to the authorities:

1) Affirm as correct Hu Yaobang's views on democracy and freedom;
2) Admit that the campaigns against spiritual pollution and bourgeois liberalisation had been wrong;
3) Publish information on the income of state leaders and their family members;
4) End the ban on privately run newspapers and stop press censorship;
5) Increase funding for education and raise intellectuals' pay;
6) End restrictions on demonstrations in Beijing;
7) Provide objective coverage of students in official media.

To those of us who live in a democracy, all these would seem fair and reasonable. But China was (and remains today) a one-party state. The idea of objective media coverage, or of wider democracy, was unthinkable. The publication of the wealth of individual party members would reveal the massive extent to which corruption had become endemic at the senior levels of the hierarchy, and that too was taboo. All the student demands would in some way or another have threatened the monopoly of power that the party enjoyed.

In May the Soviet leader Mikhail Gorbachev was due in Beijing for talks. This was deeply symbolic, since the USSR and China, the two rival Marxist states, had not spoken to each other at such a high level for over three decades – the Sino–Soviet 'split' of which Richard Nixon had taken advantage in his own diplomacy with China back in the 1970s. The presence of hundreds of thousands of student demonstrators in the main square of Beijing – Tiananmen had been such for hundreds of years – was a major loss of face for the Chinese government.

However, rather than going away, the students increased their activity by initiating hunger strikes, which upped the emotional element of the protests considerably. These new methods began on May 13th, and by this time there were probably over 300,000 protesters in the square. Gorbachev's visit also meant that the world media would be there, as the students realised, so when Gorbachev held talks with the Chinese leadership on May 16th, journalists from every part of the globe were present not just for the discussions but also to witness the students protesting in such vast numbers. The embarrassment of the government and senior party leadership was total.

Nor did the party hierarchy agree among themselves about what to do with the students. The party boss, Zhao Ziyang, was in favour of arbitration and at least being seen to talk to the protesters, in order, if anything, to better lance the boil. But others, such as Premier Li Peng, were against even the smallest compromise. One of the major issues for any authoritarian or totalitarian regime (either of these slightly different terms could be used of China in 1989) is that of legitimacy. As there is no democracy, how is your rule legitimate in the eyes of the people? Economic prosperity was supposed to have solved this problem – or so the party leaders had hoped. But with more personal wealth, people were now demanding something not on offer – political freedom as well.

The hunger strikes had galvanised ordinary Chinese across the nation. Protests were no longer limited just to Beijing but to cities the length and breadth of the land. Some *million* citizens were now protesting in Beijing itself. What scared the party hierarchy considerably was the fact that many ordinary workers were now joining in the protests and very publicly. China was supposed to be a 'workers' state' and now the working class was showing dangerous signs of solidarity with the students. Junior party cadres were also now seen supporting the demonstrations, and even more scarily – from the point of view of the party – so were members of the People's Liberation Army (PLA), the Chinese armed forces. The situation was looking as if it could get out of control.

As a consequence the party leadership was split. On May 19th Zhao Ziyang decided to go and reason with the students in the square. From a rational viewpoint this was a sensible thing to do, to show that the country's rulers were at least listening. But others in the hierarchy, and most notably Deng himself, were horrified. This could, they feared, bring back the chaos of the Cultural Revolution crashing upon their heads, and maybe even lead to civil war. A military solution to the protesters seemed to the national leadership the only way out. As a result, PLA divisions were sent to the capital, with not a few of the soldiers being those born hundreds or even thousands of miles away from Beijing, with the idea that if real violence erupted they would not be shooting their own friends and family.

While all this was happening some commentators from the West, getting very excited at events in the square, even contemplated aloud that this could be the end of Communist rule in China. All this was well meant and doubtless sincere. But it played right into the hands of the party hard men, who feared exactly that outcome. And so such talk actually made more likely the massacre that was now being planned as the only solution to the problem. Zhao Ziyang was stripped of his party membership and sacked as general secretary.

On May 20th martial law was proclaimed in Beijing. But as those who have seen the iconic photo of a protester trying to stop a tank will recall (the picture was taken on June 5th, but the point applies), it was very hard for the army to get into the centre of the city without mass bloodshed. The situation was getting more tense by the day, if not the hour, and the party leadership knew that by now the eyes of the whole world were on Beijing.

In imperial times emperors had issued rescripts of key policies, and on June 1st the Premier Li Peng proclaimed one of his own. It was plain, he argued, that the protesters were causing turmoil and that ruthless means were the only way of solving the problem. This was a clear indication to ordinary members of the party around the whole country – some 400 cities had seen protests of some kind or another by now – that violence was the only way forward. The elder statesmen of the party met on June 2nd with those members of the politburo who had not been sacked, and resolved to send in the troops. It was now only a matter of time before the killing would begin.

The troops moved in from all over the city on the night of June 3rd. Shooting began straight away and by the early hours of the morning the PLA was in the square itself, the students having maintained their position of non-violence (though some ordinary citizens threw rocks in anger). It is heavily disputed how many of the innocent victims were slaughtered on the June 3rd–4th. The government admitted to somewhat over 200 while reputable Western journalists reckoned that the death toll might have been nearer to 800. And either way, thousands of protesters were injured, with the city's hospitals rapidly filling up with casualties throughout the night.

Eventually the entire square was cleared. Deng proclaimed that the injured or killed PLA soldiers were the true martyrs, and dissent around the country was now ruthlessly suppressed. Some of the students managed to escape not just Beijing but the country altogether, getting to Hong Kong and from there to the USA. But most were nowhere as lucky and were imprisoned. The movement had failed.

Today the situation is politically much the same as in 1989, except that perhaps the current leadership is genuine in its wish to stamp out the corruption that so marred China in the past: at least that is a real improvement. But otherwise the country remains a one-party-rule Communist state, with the discrepancy between rich and poor being possibly wider than ever before. Dissent is crushed as always. Internet access is heavily censored, for instance, by what is nicknamed 'the Great Fire Wall of China'. The 2010 Nobel Peace Prize winner Liu Xiaobo remains in prison for his beliefs. So was it worth the cost? The answer is a hard one to call – except that, in another part of the world in 1989 another Communist regime, that in East Germany, had to make a similar decision, one that by then was called the Tiananmen Option. They decided against killing their own people – and were promptly ejected from power, a lesson that the leadership in China have not forgotten . . .

POLL TAX PROTESTS

(1989)

No one likes paying taxes, but most of us believe that they are a good idea so long as they are fair. In Britain and Western Europe taxes pay for enormous amounts of things from which we benefit – schools, hospitals, the collection of litter, the police – and by and large we do not begrudge what we gain back in terms of the services paid for out of government tax revenue.

But what if the tax is unfair? Or what if the majority of us obliged to pay it by law regard it as being unfair?

The British have traditionally never liked what are called 'poll taxes' or taxes levied upon us as individuals that do not take into account our income or ability to pay. My ancestors were involved in active protests against such forms of taxation in Wales some two centuries ago, and many an English (and possibly therefore American, Canadian, Australian or New Zealand) person today descends from common folk who revolted against the government of King Richard II in 1381 – the Peasants' Revolt.

In the 1980s the then Conservative government, under Margaret Thatcher, strongly disliked the way in which local councils seemed, according to Thatcherite ideology, to be profligate in the way they both raised and spent the money of local taxpayers. So a 'Community Charge' was introduced whereby everyone would pay the identical tax, as individuals. Local tax had hitherto been based essentially on property values – the more valuable your house or apartment, the more you paid. And under the old rates system many were exempt from any payments altogether.

While this might have seemed fair and fiscally responsible to those drawing up the new tax, it appeared outrageous to scores of voters across the country. A simple example is where your author then lived. I had an apartment with just me living in it. Two neighbours inhabited an apartment of identical size. Under the rates system they jointly paid the identical rates that I did for my apartment. But under the 'Community Charge' they paid *twice* as much as I did – I was an individual living in my apartment and they were a couple, so since everyone was taxed as a person and not as a property owner, they now had to pay double the amount that I owed, even though their apartment and mine were exactly the same size.

So I benefited from the 'Community Charge', or poll tax as it rightly came to be nicknamed, since historically that is what it was, and my neighbours were left worse off than before.

But the key thing about a poll tax was that it was a flat rate and bore no relationship to the incomes people earned or the level of their wealth. So a low-waged road sweeper would pay the same as a hedge fund billionaire, or as many put it at the time, a duke would pay the same as a dustman. Nowhere was your ability to pay taken into account. Two people in a large house paid less than four people living in a shack.

Needless to say this struck the majority of people as grossly unfair. The government also made the tactical mistake of introducing it first in Scotland. While the Conservatives enjoyed a large parliamentary majority of seats in England, in Scotland they held hardly any seats at all. So the Scots saw this as an English Conservative government imposing an unfair tax on Labour-, SNP- or Liberal Democrat-majority voting Scotland, creating a dislike of Westminster government with implications that live with us today.

Major demonstrations began in England in the autumn of 1989, but the biggest of all of them was a protest that turned into a riot, the so-called 'Battle of Trafalgar Square' in London on March 31st 1990. As always, exact numbers are disputed, but it is possible that somewhere around 200,000 protesters were in Trafalgar Square, at the heart of London. What started peacefully escalated into a riot, and it became necessary for mounted police to charge against the rioters in order to restore order.

In essence one could say that the poll tax protesters lost the battle but won the war, and in ways that they did not expect or wish. Conservative MPs were already becoming unhappy at what they felt was Mrs Thatcher's loss of popular instinct and increasingly domineering nature. Above all she no longer seemed to be the electoral asset that she had once been – the Labour Party lead in the opinion polls looked insurmountable.

192 | Christopher Catherwood

She had been challenged for the leadership of her party in 1989, and riots in the streets about a tax that seemed unfair was not helping her reputation. When in late 1990 she alienated many key MPs in her party over another issue – relations with Europe – the political daggers were unsheathed and she was deposed as leader and therefore as prime minister.

The new prime minister, John Major, appointed Thatcher's arch-opponent Michael Heseltine as relevant minister for local government taxation. The latter introduced legislation that abolished the hated 'Community Charge' and returned to a banded-tax arrangement much more similar to the old system of rates. With Thatcher gone and the poll tax ceasing to exist, the Conservatives won the general election in 1992. Their victory is more complex than that, but the U-turn on tax robbed the Labour opposition of a major weapon. Many of the poll tax protesters had been on the left, if not actual Trotskyites as some of the organisers had been, and the result of their demonstrations ended up with five more years of Conservative government – not something they had anticipated. But local tax is fairer again than during that brief period under Thatcher and once more the lessons of the Peasants' Revolt of 1381 had been learnt, this time without anything like the violence of the Middle Ages.

THE PRAGUE SPRING AND
VELVET REVOLUTION

(1989)

Turn the last two numerals of the year 1968 another way and you can get 1989.

As the British actor Michael Caine is often supposed to say, 'not a lot of people know that'. But they do in Central Europe, and in particular in what we now call the Czech Republic. So too do all the readers of the very exciting contemporary accounts written in 1989 about the extraordinary events of that epochal year. In particular there is the account *We the People* by Timothy Garton Ash, who witnessed the key happenings in person, as did all those glued to their television screens and the reporting by John Simpson of the protests that changed history. Many people celebrate 1989, the overthrow of the Communist bloc in Europe, because of the fall of the iconic Berlin Wall. But there is a good case for saying that the protests in Czechoslovakia that same autumn are in fact even more important, and are proof that peaceful protests can indeed prevail even over the worst of tyrannies.

To understand what is called the 'Velvet Revolution' in Prague and other parts of the country it would help to look a little further back in Czech history. For we cannot see events such as those of 1989 if we wrest them out of context. Many tried to do so in 2011 in the Middle East, where, as we shall see, the cultural, political and economic background of the countries involved in the latter protests could not be more different from those that in Central Europe freed themselves from Soviet oppression in 1989.

After 1918 many new countries were formed from the ruins of the Austro-Hungarian, Russian and Ottoman Empires. One of these was Czechoslovakia, an entity that had never existed before, constructed principally out of the Bohemian and Moravian provinces of Austria and the predominantly Slovak portions of the old Hungarian kingdom. So far as the Czech/Bohemian part was concerned, there had been a long history of economic prosperity, comparative political freedom (there was a Bohemian parliament, albeit not an independent one) and a very high degree of literacy and education.

As a result, whereas many of the other new post-1918 states, such as restored Poland, or the expanded Romanian kingdom, swiftly became autocracies of one kind or another, Czechoslovakia remained a beacon of democracy, freedom and the rule of law. And as Czechs would remind people, Prague is further west than Vienna, so while Czechoslovakia was a Central European country, it was, in the proper sense, really part of Western Europe.

Tragically, in 1938, Britain and France cynically betrayed Czechoslovakia at a conference in Munich, abandoning the one democracy in the region to Adolf Hitler and the Nazis. In 1939 the rump of the shattered state was split, with the Czech part becoming part of the Reich, and Slovakia a puppet Fascist regime under Nazi tutelage. Foolishly in 1945 the Allied command prevented the swashbuckling American general, Patton, from liberating Prague from the Germans. So it was Red Army troops from the USSR that took Czechoslovakia and after just three years, in 1948, Stalin engineered a coup that abolished democracy and put the nation firmly under Soviet rule from Moscow.

So for twenty years Czechoslovakia was an oppressed Warsaw Pact Communist-controlled state (the Warsaw Pact being the Soviet bloc equivalent of NATO). The president, Antonín Novotný, did what Moscow wanted. Thousands of innocent Czechs and Slovaks were imprisoned and some killed. Freedom did not exist – officially. Unofficially there was an underground of brave writers and dissidents, many made known through the bravery of similar people in the West who supported them, such as the Czech-born British playwright Tom Stoppard, who publicised their plight. But with the danger of World War III always possible if NATO tried to do anything to liberate the millions behind the Iron Curtain, there was nothing that the Western democracies could do to help.

By the end of 1967 even the sclerotic Soviet leadership knew that the Czechoslovak regime was widely hated. They decided to change the local leadership. In January 1968 they appointed a new general secretary of the Communist Party – the post in the Soviet bloc countries that really mattered – and so a young Slovak party loyalist called Alexander Dubček found himself in power. And then in April Novotný was deposed, and an actually well-liked and revered war hero, General Ludvík Svoboda, became president.

The events that unfolded are often known as the Prague Spring, but in reality they began when Dubček assumed office in January and lasted until August when Warsaw Pact armies led by the USSR invaded the country and crushed all dissent.

Ironically, in retrospect, back in 1968 Dubček was only trying to do in Czechoslovakia what Mikhail Gorbachev attempted in the USSR after assuming control in 1985. Dubček did not want to overthrow Communism, since he was loyal to it ideologically and to its precepts. But what he wanted to achieve was to give it a 'human face' and to legitimate it in the eyes of ordinary people by giving them many cultural and personal freedoms while keeping the Communist Party essentially still in charge.

So for a brief time – not just the spring in the literal sense but a genuine awakening period – artistic and intellectual freedom were allowed to flower. Playwrights such as Václav Havel were allowed to write controversial plays that did not worship the Communist system.

But for Leonid Brezhnev and the hardliners in Moscow even a limited amount of free speech was too much. Dubček was asked to curtail the newly granted liberties and reimpose Soviet orthodoxy. When he bravely refused the USSR ordered all the other countries of the Warsaw Pact to invade Czechoslovakia and crush the dissent. President Svoboda, while personally empathetic to the changes, naturally feared carnage and civil war, so ordered the Czechoslovak Army not to resist the invaders. Dubček was overthrown and another Slovak, this time the hardliner Gustáv

Husák, assumed power. However, it was not as bad as 1956 in Hungary, when Imre Nagy, the national hero, was shot. Dubček was released and became the caretaker of a small forest reserve, alive but very much out of power.

For the next twenty years Czechoslovakia became one of the most oppressive of all the Soviet bloc regimes, with all dissent crushed and driven even further underground. (Your author was arrested on one of his visits to dissidents during this time, but thankfully released . . .) In theory the USSR signed up in 1977 to the Helsinki Accords that permitted freedom of speech, but in practice the oppression continued. Brave dissidents such as Havel were imprisoned (in his case more than once, including 1979–1983). Many protesters ended up in menial jobs, such as lavatory cleaners, or were forced into exile.

But in 1985 major change occurred, and in an unexpected place – the Soviet Union. Mikhail Gorbachev, hitherto a loyal apparatchik, was elected general secretary of the Communist Party, and to the astonishment of everyone began to try to reform and legitimise Communism *from within*. So increasingly the hitherto despotic USSR was granting more change and openness – what Gorbachev called perestroika (literally 'reconstructing', rebuilding the Soviet Union in new and dynamic ways) and glasnost (or 'openness', getting rid of the culture of secrecy) – than the repressive satellite states such as Czechoslovakia and the German Democratic Republic, a highly unusual turn of events.

This context is vital. Gorbachev was in Beijing in 1989 on a State Visit, and as we saw looking at the Tiananmen Square protests, the Chinese government ended the occupation by shooting the protesters without mercy. Had anyone other than

198 | Christopher Catherwood

Gorbachev been in power in Moscow, the freedom movements across the Iron Curtain countries could have been crushed completely and history would have been very different. But he was the person who made the decisions, and his refusal to use armed force and military violence to suppress dissent meant that the Soviet satellite regimes in places such as Hungary and Czechoslovakia were on their own. They would have to emulate the Chinese and kill their own people. With no support from the USSR they rejected that option.

So slowly but surely Soviet despotism in Europe began to unravel. We look separately at East Germany and Poland. But the events in Hungary, which neighboured Czechoslovakia to the south, also made a huge difference.

After the brutal repression of 1956 the regime there decided on what was soon nicknamed 'goulash Communism'. In return for utter political loyalty to the USSR, and unquestioning Communist rule, ordinary citizens were allowed more individual freedoms than in some of the other Warsaw Pact countries. By 1989 the Hungarian regime realised that its own legitimacy was fading fast. So in October the Communist Party abolished itself, changed its name to the Socialist Party, ended one-party rule, and instituted democracy. All this was done without a shot being fired and entirely from within, an extraordinary turn of events for which the Hungarians have had too little credit. Similar changes began to take place, as we see elsewhere, and so by November 1989 the ruling Czechoslovak regime realised that it was now in real danger.

Of the making of conspiracy theories there is no end, and many exist in relation to the fall of the Iron Curtain, so that in some ways it is hard to know what *really* happened behind closed doors. But there is one possible scenario that *if* true, might apply to this story. One of Gorbachev's friends from student days was the leading Czech Communist, Zdeněk Mlynář. But the latter became disillusioned with that ideology and exiled himself to Austria. In 1989, because of his links to Gorbachev, some in the party in Prague thought that if he returned, he could institute 'Communism with a human face', the very ideology rejected in 1968 but now the norm in the USSR. But he refused, and so the regime found itself without a Plan B.

So when students started to protest on November 16th 1989, a chain of events was set into motion that within four weeks led to the overthrow of one of the most tyrannical governments in Europe. And rather than Mlynář, the beneficiary was an unlikely politician, the playwright dissident Václav Havel, whose Civic Forum movement sprang into the gap left by pro-reform Communists. This created a most unlikely revolution, entirely peaceful and consisting of writers, intellectuals, actors, students, rock stars, and, as Timothy Garton Ash reminds us, the occasional worker. Much of what followed was planned in the Magic Lantern Theatre in Prague, and many of the events were almost a sixties 'happening' in their tone, but with politically and dramatically different results. Strikes took place, but with people in the West knowing more about them than those in the country itself, since state television ruthlessly suppressed the news.

By November 20th the more realistic members of the ruling politburo understood that things should change, among them being the prime minister, Ladislav Adamec. But the hardliners in the party still had the majority, and hoped that the disturbances could be suppressed. Adamec, torn between a rock and a hard place, tried to negotiate with Civic Forum while insisting on one-party rule. Events soon made this option impossible, as by November 21st, hundreds of thousands of people were protesting on the streets of Prague and of the Slovak capital Bratislava. The famous Wenceslas Square in Prague became the centre of protest and of popular feeling against the Communist regime.

Some in the party still argued for repression, and of calling on the so-called 'People's Militias' to suppress the demonstrations. But like the similar politburo discussions in Berlin, the decision was made *not* to use force, and, as in East Germany, this was to prove a tipping point. (The army refused to let itself be used for violence.) There would be no Tiananmen in Wenceslas Square.

Consequently, events began to spiral out of the control of the Communists. Workers, supposedly the lynchpin of any Marxist regime, began to boo leading officials. On November 24th, again as in Berlin, the party tried to reshuffle itself in the hope that more moderate Communists might perform the trick of reducing tensions and stay in power. Karel Urbánek was installed as new general secretary, but it was as elsewhere, too little and too late.

One of the most iconic and moving acts of that day was the appearance on the balcony of the theatre overlooking the square of Alexander Dubček. His moment had gone – his form of Communism was finished – but he would, once the revolution was completed, become speaker of the newly and democratically elected Czechoslovak Parliament, in December.

Civic Forum and the protesters around Havel now had the workers on their side, and a general strike was proclaimed for November 27th – over three-quarters of the people took part and paralysed the state. By this time there were over 800,000 people demonstrating for the regime to fall, and chanting 'Havel for the Castle', the famous Renaissance Hradčany Castle from which Bohemia and then Czechoslovakia had been ruled for centuries.

So by November 29th the Federal Assembly bowed to the inevitable and abolished the so-called 'leading role' of the Communist Party in national affairs. By December it was all over, and the first genuinely free government since 1948 took power. Václav Havel was sworn in as president on December 29th, the former prisoner now the head of state of a newly liberated country.

No one had been killed – something truly extraordinary in the light of what could so easily have happened. In 1993 Czechoslovakia split into its component parts – the Czech Republic (the historic Bohemia and Moravia) and Slovakia. Again this happened without bloodshed, so unlike the disintegration around the same time of nearby Yugoslavia, in which tens of thousands of people were killed throughout the 1990s as that country also broke up. It was an extraordinary achievement. Now the Czech Republic and Slovakia are members of the European Union and of NATO, and the world is a freer and better place. The brave protesters of November 1989 had succeeded beyond their dreams.

UKRAINE FROM THE ORANGE REVOLUTION TO WAR

(1991, 2004 and 2014)

On July 17th 2014 nearly 300 entirely innocent people, many from the Netherlands and Britain, were slaughtered in the skies when a missile hit the plane in which they were flying, they thought, from Amsterdam to Kuala Lumpur, thousands of miles away in Malaysia. Many of the bodies – including those of children – have never been fully recovered.

What caused this massacre in the air? Why had the area over which they were flying in blissful ignorance become a war zone? And what had their deaths to do with protests in the historic Ukrainian city of Kiev back in 2004 and then again in early 2014? To gain a proper understanding we need to go back in time and grasp fully the context in which both the protests and the mass murder took place.

What is good news for one person or country is bad news for another.

Of few places in the world is this adage truer than in the countries that make up the former Soviet Union. In theory, the USSR was not nationalist but a genuine federation of states united in their love for and adherence to Marxist–Leninist Communism. But in practice, although individual rulers such as Stalin (who was ethnically a Georgian, from the Caucasus) were non-Russian, the USSR was in reality the old Tsarist Russian Empire under another name.

Therefore, from that viewpoint, the fall of the USSR in late 1991, and its replacement by a much looser Confederation of Independent States (CIS), was an unmitigated disaster and national humiliation on a grand scale. Today in the Russian Federation there is much nostalgia for Stalin, and for the certainties of Soviet rule, even though by any normal standard those decades were some of the most bloodthirsty and politically repressive ever seen in human history. It is reckoned by some that twenty *million* people were put to death in the Soviet political prison camp system, known by many as the Gulag Archipelago (and made famous by Russian novelists such as the Nobel Literature Prize winner Alexander Solzhenitsyn).

Thus from the Russian vantage point, the accession both to the EU and to NATO of countries that had been Soviet Republics, such as Estonia, Latvia and Lithuania, and the moving into a more pro-Western position by even Stalin's own home state, Georgia, were highly dangerous developments, bringing the NATO border, say, with Estonia, only a comparatively few miles away from the former Russian capital, St Petersburg.

In the West, we forget this, and with very good reason. Suppose that you are a Pole or an Estonian. Your country had been seized by the USSR in 1939–1940, and independence and freedom ruthlessly suppressed, in the latter case for well over half a century (1940–1991). Now, at last, you can rejoin Western Europe, and an alliance that guarantees that the world's biggest superpower, the USA, will defend you and your nation against any armed attempt by the Russians to invade and reconquer you. You are politically and economically free and militarily safe. Your old oppressor is powerless against you, and cannot ever again simply abolish your culture, your heritage and your very freedom itself. What could be better than that?

So two very different perspectives on the *same* set of events: the disintegration of the Soviet bloc in Central Europe in 1989, and the dissolution of the USSR itself in 1991. For one group – the Russians – utter degradation and humiliation, for another (millions of Estonians, Poles, Czechs, Lithuanians and others), joy at liberation and a happy welcome to their true European home.

However, there is a complication, one created deliberately by Stalin, and with dire consequences for us today, with even the risk of international war all over again, a century after the start of the carnage of World War I in 1914.

Stalin, being a Georgian himself, knew full well that the millions of new subjects that the USSR had acquired did not love their Soviet rulers in Moscow. While the USSR was theoretically an international, multi-ethnic federation, the Russians, by far the biggest nation grouping, were the effective rulers. And so placing thousands of ethnic Russians in the new

Soviet republics – the three Baltic states, Ukraine, Belarus, and the 'Stans' such as Kazakhstan – ensured that there would always be a minority utterly loyal to Moscow and to the Soviet Union.

While everything was ruled from Moscow this did not matter. But once those countries became genuinely independent, this suddenly became a major issue.

Remember any history that you might have studied about 1919–1939 and the causes of the Second World War? One of the key factors was the presence of large German minorities in the newly created states, such as Czechoslovakia, Poland, the Baltic States and others. Hitler was able to use these German minorities to claim large swathes of the territory of his neighbours, most notoriously that of Czechoslovakia in late 1938.

In 1945 much of this issue was solved by the complete defeat of Nazi Germany and the expulsion in the immediate aftermath of the war of millions of ethnic Germans from lands their ancestors had inhabited for centuries, but whose governments regarded them understandably as a major security threat. Millions were forced to flee and move to Germany and not a few died during the process of what we would today describe as 'ethnic cleansing'.

However, in 1991 the USSR had not lost a war but simply imploded politically from within. Millions of Russians, both in the newly independent states such as Latvia or the Ukraine, had an outcome imposed upon them that they had not chosen, and which now separated them legally and politically from their fellow ethnic Russians in the Russian Federation itself, the rump state left after the USSR's demise. Worse still, both Stalin and later on Khrushchev had redrawn the borders of the USSR member states in a way that placed millions of ethnic Russians nominally outside the Russian Federation – which is what happened in the Ukraine. With the Soviet Union in one piece this was effectively irrelevant, but when, say, Ukraine and Latvia became independent, vast numbers of ethnic Russians now found themselves as minorities in countries that often had bad memories both of Tsarist Russian and then Soviet rule. The worst example of this was Ukraine.

The Ukraine or does one say simply Ukraine? That definite article can make a huge difference and unwary Westerners can employ it without realising the very serious political implications involved.

Ukraine or, to use a similar word from the former Yugoslavia, the Krajina, simply means 'border country'. But the border between what and whom? That has become a very important question for which people are dying as this book is being written. It is at the heart of what is happening in Ukraine/the Ukraine in our very own times.

Back in 873, Kiev was at the heart of a wholly new part of the world – the Rus, a region we now know as Russia. But over the course of centuries borders changed and much of what is today's Russia was conquered by the Mongol hordes from Asia. One country they failed to capture was the infant Poland, which in the fourteenth century combined together with the recently Christianised Lithuania to form a unique elected monarchy, the Polish–Lithuanian Commonwealth. For long periods Kiev became a city within this kingdom, as anyone who reads the definitive books by Norman Davies can discover in more detail. But by the eighteenth century the once mighty Commonwealth had become a shadow of its original self and, as we saw earlier, was split in three by predatory neighbours, effectively to vanish until the end of World War I.

So no such country as the Ukraine existed until 1918. But a very large *region* existed, a contested borderland between Poland–Lithuania to the West and Tsarist Russia to the east – and Ukraine is the Slavic word that denotes that border area. If it is *the* Ukraine it is not a place in its own right but somewhere contested between two neighbours. If it is simply Ukraine, without article, it is a country in its own right.

Come 1991 the nation gained independence under the very ethnically shaky borders granted to it by first Stalin and then by Kruschev, in the latter case as late as the 1950s. Crimea, for example, had been the last vestige of the old Mongolian/Tartar Empire, and up to 1945 had a substantial Tartar (and Muslim) population that was exiled by Stalin for their supposed sympathies to the Nazis. The peninsula was conquered by *Russians* under Catherine the Great and was always seen as Russia's outlet through the Black Sea to the Mediterranean.

And much of the eastern part of Ukraine was ethnically Russian, with the western area calling itself Ukrainian, but historically all part of the vast former Polish–Lithuanian Commonwealth for centuries. Indeed part of today's Ukraine was Polish from 1920 (when Polish forces defeated the Communist invaders) until 1939, when Stalin recouped much lost territory in his deal that year with Hitler.

So what is Ukraine? And does it go in a Western (and thus pro-EU and pro-NATO) direction? Or do its real loyalties lie with Russia? And if you are a Russian, do you want an EU and NATO country on your border? Or do you want to reunite with your lost Russian motherland? If you are a Ukrainian, do you want to join Poland and Lithuania, two nations that have successfully rediscovered their European roots and gained independence in the process?

What are therefore ostensibly political arguments, about who should rule the country, about what to do with corruption, about foreign trade, are therefore in reality what one might call 'presentation issues', with the *real* debate being based upon identity and about to whom the country truly belongs.

This was therefore the cause of the Orange Revolution in the country, between November 2004 and January 2005. (Many such movements at that time were awarded colours, and the Ukraine's was orange.) Enormous protests broke out in the capital Kiev and other cities on November 22nd, about who had won the recent presidential election. Most people in the western part of the country thought that the true winner was their candidate, Viktor Yushchenko, whereas those in the more Russian-leaning east felt that the ostensible winner, Viktor Yanukovych, was both the overt and genuine winner.

Huge protests took place by those supporting Yushchenko, who was also the candidate against corruption and who opposed the kind of oppressive links with Russia from which the neighbouring state of Belarus was increasingly suffering, with democracy thus being endangered. All kinds of accusations were hurled by one side against the other and the demonstrations reflected the strong views on both sides of the debate. The Supreme Court came to the rescue on December 3rd. So massive had the electoral fraud been, they decreed, that a run-off election would have to be held, in the hope that the matter could be decided by peaceful ballot. On January 10th 2005 they announced that Yushchenko had in fact won the new vote, and by 51.99% to 44.20% for Yanukovych, who conceded defeat. The Orange Revolution was over.

However, life is not always that simple. In 2010 there was the next regular election and this time Yanukovych won on the final ballot, over Yulia Tymoshenko, by 48.95% of the votes to 45.47%, an incredibly small margin, but this time allowed without the protests of late 2004.

Yanukovych was from the pro-Russian side of the country, and as well as serving for a time as prime minister, he had been Governor of Donetsk, a very strongly ethnically Russian region. Needless to say, this was reflected in his policies as president, taking the nation away from a Western orientation to one closer to the Russian Federation and its leader Vladimir Putin.

The straw that broke the camel's back came in November 2013. There had already been tensions in the western part of the country, and when the president decided to cancel a possible EU–Ukrainian Association Agreement (usually the preliminary step for a nation seeking eventually to join the EU), thousands of Ukrainians took to the streets of the capital in Kiev in angry protest. The heart of the city was the Maidan, a square that, like so many protests across the world (Tiananmen in China, Tahrir Square in Egypt), swiftly took on iconic significance.

Clashes with the police soon began, but the protesters stood their ground and maintained their position in the square for weeks on end. Numbers, as so often, are notoriously difficult to guess, but substantially over half a million people might not be a bad estimate, albeit with numbers declining slightly as the freezing cold of a Ukrainian winter discouraged some supporters from attending. Because of the pro-EU sympathies of many of the protesters, the square was nicknamed the 'Euromaidan' by some.

What began peacefully inevitably escalated, with some quite violent riots breaking out in December 2013, with overall casualties possibly rising into the hundreds of killed or wounded. By 2014 it was clear that the protests were escalating into a full-scale demand for the president to be overthrown, with the widescale corruption of the ruling regime now also at the forefront of many minds. In February it is estimated that as many as a hundred protesters were killed as the riots became widespread across the country, with most of the casualties occurring in Kiev but with demonstrations in many of the major cities.

By February 18th–23rd 2014 the original protests had transformed into a national revolution. The killings motivated those in the parliament on the side of the protesters to take action. President Yanukovych did his best to try to negotiate his survival in power, but on February 21st he realised that for him the game was probably up. He first fled to a city favourable to him and from there to Russia, where he reappeared on the 28th, protesting against events back in Kiev.

The parliament had already chosen an interim president on February 22nd, and on May 25th 2014 Petro Poroshenko, a successful confectionary billionaire, was elected president with over 54% of the votes on the first ballot.

As of the time of writing he is still the president. But many parts of the eastern Ukraine, those inhabited by ethnic Russians, refused to recognise his legitimacy. The actual involvement of

212 | Christopher Catherwood

shadowy Russian security forces, mercenaries and others in what now happened is still disputed, though most commentators in the West seem to agree that President Putin has been active in the support of the Russian separatists and that actual members of the Russian armed services are fighting alongside the rebels against Ukrainian government forces. It is a low-intensity war in all but name, and since the Malaysian flight in which so many innocent people lost their lives was flying over rebel-controlled territory, many seem to suspect either Russian forces or rebels with access to Russian army missile launchers as the most likely perpetrators of the massacre, quite possibly, though, as a truly hideous mistake.

Ukraine suffered greatly from its bold attempts to break away from the Russian stranglehold. The Crimean Peninsula, part of legitimate Ukrainian territory since the 1950s, was seized back by rebels with Russian aid, an act that led many worldwide to protest at the biggest land grab in Europe since the Nazis back in the 1930s.

Once again perception is everything! For those of us living in the West, the Ukrainian people have found their voice, taken active steps against rampant corruption, overthrown a semi-dictator whose actions were dominated by hated foreigners, and in the process rediscovered democracy and freedom. From the Russian viewpoint, however, a legitimately elected president was overthrown in a Western-backed illegal coup, and the forces of NATO are now right on the borders of the Russian Federation itself thanks to their puppet president in Kiev.

Needless to say, there is a gigantic difference between these two perceptions of recent events! Most of us in the West would be more sympathetic to the former rather than to the latter. From either perspective, though, war has returned to Europe and at the time of writing, fighting continues – despite numerous failed ceasefire attempts – in the eastern part of the country. The rebels no longer regard themselves as Ukrainians but as long-lost Russians wishing permanently to return home (the Crimea has been formally annexed back to the Russian Federation). What will have happened by the time that you read this book is unclear.

So a protest against a political decision has broken a country and put it on the path to war, with collateral damage costing the lives of hundreds of British and Dutch victims. As we see in the next entry, be careful what you wish for!

BE CAREFUL WHAT YOU WISH FOR: THE ARAB SPRING TO THE ARAB WINTER

(2011)

As the old saying goes, be careful what you wish for . . .

One of the dangers of contemporary history is that events overtake the writer all too quickly. The classic example of this is the so-called 'Arab Spring' of 2011, which all too rapidly became the 'Arab Winter' for many of the participants. The bright hopes for freedom of the protesters in Tahrir Square in 2011 have now led to another military-style regime in Egypt itself (albeit one proclaiming itself a democracy), some 200,000 innocent people slaughtered in Syria, and two million Syrian refugees around the Middle East.

Events might change things even before you read this book! One good piece of news is that Tunisia, where the original demonstrations began in late 2010, is the one success of the whole 'Arab Spring' movement. There, a successful transition to genuine democracy took place, including the presidential election at the end of 2014. Sadly the rest of the news is not so great . . .

There is general agreement that one of the most seismic shifts in any region of the world in recent times began with the self-immolation of a street vendor in Tunisia called Mohamed Bouazizi in December 2010. The man who died in a lone protest against corruption was of no great importance, yet his death was to light the fuse for a whole series of street protests that has convulsed the Arab world ever since; in the same way in which Gavrilo Princip could never have anticipated the millions who died in World War I when he assassinated Archduke Franz Ferdinand, the break-up of empires, the coming to power in Russia of Communism, and a second interrelated conflict a few years later in which even more millions of people were killed.

By January 2011 protests were erupting all over the Middle East North Africa or MENA region. The government in Tunisia, where all the protests had begun, was perhaps more corrupt than many similar regimes in a part of the world in which corruption was the norm. And so on January 14th 2011 the regime was overthrown.

That month the major protests also began in Egypt. This is not the richest country in the Middle East but it is by far the most populous and easily the most critical politically. On January 25th, thousands of anti-regime protestors assembled in Tahrir Square in Cairo (and in other parts of the country as well) and stayed there. By remaining they were being immensely brave, since it soon became apparent that only a Tiananmen Square solution or massacre could move them.

It turned out to be crucial. Suddenly people lost their fear of the dreaded Secret Police. It became increasingly apparent too that the army, the bastion of power in Egypt, would not order the slaughter of its own fellow citizens. But as one adviser to the British government on Middle East issues commented afterwards, media coverage, while comprehensive, was deeply misleading. Television news had photogenic English-speaking, university-educated and head-uncovered women in its bulletins. Such interviewees represented genuine and deeply held convictions. They might also have reflected the majority opinion in the crowd. But they were utterly atypical of the people of Egypt themselves. Most Egyptians are peasants living in the countryside, equally opposed to the corruption of the Mubarak regime, but people who believe in a very different destiny for their nation than the Western media-friendly people in the Square.

In the short term the liberals protesting in Cairo got their way. On February 11th Mubarak resigned, making way for an interim government that, ominously in retrospect, essentially drew its power from the army – the SCAF (Supreme Council of the Armed Forces). The road to democracy was, in theory at least, now beginning. On March 3rd his prime minister resigned as well.

In Egypt, this part of the transition was comparatively peaceful. The same, however, did not necessarily apply elsewhere. Many of the monarchies did well – in Jordan and in Morocco the rulers also had the legitimacy of bona fide descent from the Prophet Muhammad. But in Bahrain the dynasty was Sunni, ruling over a majority Shiite population. Bahrain is only a short bridge away from Saudi Arabia, and under the cover of the Gulf Consultative Council, Saudi troops were sent in to crush the democracy protests in the country. The idea of a Shiite regime was scary not just for the Sunni/Wahhabi House of Saud but also for the Americans, with a fleet based in the area, there to keep an eye on nearby Iran. Western support for freedom and democracy is, alas, as many in the region now realised, not always consistent, and sometimes outright hypocritical.

In Libya riots against the Gaddafi regime erupted on February 15th, in Benghazi. His regime was hated for its oppression and corruption. Libya is a wholly artificial state put together as a result of Western colonialism. East and West Libya are to all intents and purposes separate countries (and, one could argue, parts of the south are, in essence, more African than Middle Eastern). The natural pre-Italian former divide now became a major factor in the Libyan situation. Not only that, but Gaddafi was no Mubarak, as he was quite happy to kill his own people. Demonstrations quickly escalated into a civil war.

This time the West was able to intervene, principally France and Britain, the two countries whose previous involvement in the region, in Suez in 1956, had been such a disaster. More successfully, in 2003 Britain (and France) played a key role in persuading Gaddafi to decommission his country's nuclear weapons – the USA was also involved.

This time around, in 2011, the USA, while carefully not taking the lead, allowed the Libyan protesters and Britain and France to proceed, and the West was, through skilful use of UN motions, able to take sides in the civil war. By August the conflict was over, with the capture of the capital, Tripoli, by rebel forces. Gaddafi was overthrown and captured, and died in October.

Yemen also had strife, with President Saleh overthrown. But that part of the world has had continuous conflict for decades, long before the Arab Spring, and the ongoing strife there can really only be understood in the context of a struggle between the artificial (and only partly colonial) unification of the country in the 1990s.

Demonstrations began in Syria against the oppressive Assad regime on March 15th. Here, small events have led to greater tragedy, with well over 200,000 deaths at the time of writing and *millions* of people displaced and exiled into foreign countries, bringing the chaos and instability of the Syrian conflict with them to their new homes in shanty towns around the region.

Assad, it soon became clear, would not hesitate to massacre as many of his subjects as was necessary to keep his dynasty and the minority Alawite group from which it came to power. As a result, what began as the normal pro-democracy demonstrations has transmogrified into a nightmarish civil war, based, as we shall see later, on what have been called 'existential' sectarian differences. Syria has a Sunni Muslim majority. The Alawites are in theory an offshoot of Shia Islam, but not all Muslims would recognise their brand of Islam as fully authentic. Then there is the not insubstantial Christian minority, which goes back to Bible times and is thus much older than Christianity in the West. Many Iraqi Christians fled Shiite persecution after the fall of Saddam Hussein in 2003 and went to Syria, where they would be protected. Now with the civil war there, that protection has gone.

As a result, it is now possible to argue, as some do, that the situation in Syria is a catastrophe in either direction. If Assad and his henchmen stay in power, the war continues and so does the massive slaughter. It became apparent in 2013, when President Obama opted out of the USA taking sides, that the West would intervene. In theory, chemical weapons and their use were the 'red line' that would trigger American intervention. But then when that line was crossed and many innocent civilians were gassed, the USA struck a deal with the Russian Federation to stop their use. (At the time of writing, it looks as if other kinds of gas are being used instead of those types theoretically banned.) As a result, the death toll has continued to mount.

However some nations, such as Qatar and Saudi Arabia, have not hesitated to be involved in arming the opposition. Some of the latter are, by Western standards, genuine moderates. But as the killing has escalated, jihadist soldiers from around the world have flocked to Syria, including radicalised Muslims from Britain and other Western nations. The Al-Nusra Front, for example, is close to the Al-Qaeda offshoots in Iraq. There is now little doubt that some factions of the opposition have also carried out atrocities. Furthermore, any hope for a multi-religious pluralist Syria would be non-existent if jihadist forces were to take power in Syria. And even supposing that they did gain control, other Muslim regimes would then want to do all possible to eliminate them. An Al-Qaeda takeover of Syria would not end the civil war.

The main story, though, must be in the most populous part of the MENA world, Egypt.

In October, an ominous sign appeared of what a Muslim Brotherhood-controlled Egypt might be like, when a church was destroyed. Women were protesting against human rights violations. In many parts of the world, religious minorities and women are the first to lose their rights when those of extreme or near-extreme views take over. Remember the meaning of the term of the Nigerian group Boko Haram – Western education is forbidden . . . Demonstrations took place in Tahrir Square in

November 2011, as people wanted the military junta to speed up the elections. But for whose benefit would victory come?

But the demonstrators were heard, and on January 24th 2012 the head of the SCAF, Field Marshal Tantawi, announced the lifting of the decades-old state of emergency. In theory at least, Egyptians would now be freer than they had been in a long time.

Then in May and June 2012 came the elections at last. Millions of people voted, with palpable excitement, since they realised that this would be the first honest election choice in their lifetimes. Women were voting, and the Fellahin in the countryside as much as the educated elites in Cairo and elsewhere.

The first round was inconclusive, with a rerun necessary. The hardline Salafists had done well. This should not have been at all surprising. Under Mubarak the Brotherhood had not been legal but had been permitted to undertake good works, among the poor and ill. This social work now paid major dividends, both for the Brotherhood itself and for the Salafist groups, who had also engaged in helping the underprivileged. Now was dividend time as the millions often ignored by the Western media thanked those who had aided them through hard times by voting for them at the ballot box.

The two final round candidates were Mohamed Morsi, the Brotherhood candidate, and Ahmed Shafik, a hold-over from the Mubarak regime. Mubarak himself had already been sentenced to life in prison the same month. He was unfortunate in that he had not been able to flee, but lucky that he had not been put to death by an angry lynch mob.

The presidential election itself took place on June 16th and 17th. It had clearly been a close call. On the 24th the

Electoral Commission announced that Morsi had won by a whisker. He had received 51.7% of the votes, against 48.3% for Shafik. Egypt had elected a Muslim Brotherhood member as president – a change from illegality to power in just a few months.

In some ways what is remarkable is that Shafik had so many votes and nearly won outright, given that he was so closely associated with such a discredited time in Egyptian history. It shows that some of the dispossessed and marginalised of the country must have voted for him, having opted for Islamist candidates in the first round.

On November 22nd Morsi awarded himself extra powers in order, as he put it, to protect the nation and constitution. Unlike his counterparts in Tunisia, where the winning Islamists were careful to share power in a coalition government, he started to act as if all Egyptians were on his side. So now, after the demonstrations to overthrow Mubarak, there were new protests, against the new leadership that had just been narrowly elected.

By early 2013 these protests became as large as those that had toppled Mubarak two years earlier. Once again Tahrir Square was filled with protestors. Hundreds of people were injured in the clashes with police that now followed. Was this, some feared, a situation not unlike Iran, where a hated dictator had been overthrown only to be replaced by something far worse?

Many ordinary Egyptians now felt that the 'one man, one vote, one time' prediction of which they had been afraid was coming to pass. Demonstrations against Morsi increased.

The reaction of the Brotherhood in taking power has

been the subject of comment by many people. Perhaps the best summary is by Roula Khalaf, a journalist writing in the *Financial Times* in 2014. She writes:

> Many factors contributed to the Islamists' failure in government. Without a clear enemy, the task of ensuring discipline became tougher. In office, 'moderation' dissipated as the rhetoric veered to the right. The inherent illiberalism of Islamists returned to the surface and was reinforced by an attitude that dismissed liberal opponents and catered to the Islamist base.

In Western democracies we are used to waiting, however frustrating that might be! In the Arab world this was a whole new territory, especially if no new free election might take place. Demonstrations became the way of showing dislike of the way in which Morsi and the Brotherhood were steering the country.

By June 30th 2013 these riots became serious, and once more Egypt found itself in a revolutionary environment. When the army asked Morsi to agree to changes, however, he refused. So on July 3rd he was deposed by the former, and he was arrested soon after. The brief experiment in democracy in Egypt was over.

At the time of writing it is still in a state of hiatus, but with the former commander of the Armed Forces, General Sisi, now the elected President of Egypt. Hundreds of members of the Muslim Brotherhood have been arrested, and many sentenced to death.

So, what does all this mean for the so-called 'Arab Spring'? And in relation to similar events in Europe, the parallel drawn by many Western commentators in 2011, we can see that Egypt was not Czechoslovakia in 1989, and that to expect a country with no history of democracy to behave as one, like the Czech Republic today, with well over a century of parliamentary experience, was in reality unfeasible.

Where does the term 'Arab Spring' originate? Is it even the right terminology?

Much thought has gone into this, including from players in the region itself, and whose views are therefore worth taking seriously. One of the interesting things to note, for example, is that except for Bahrain, which has a Sunni king ruling over an overwhelmingly Shia population, the monarchies have faired better than the republics. This is counter-intuitive, since one would have thought that presidents would do better than kings or emirs. But this does in fact seem to be the case, with the hereditary rulers of Morocco and Jordan surviving the storm better than their presidential counterparts elsewhere, not to mention the continued stability of monarchies in the Gulf, such as the UAE, Qatar and Oman.

Some Arab thinkers feel it better to talk in terms of two 'Arab Awakenings', of which this is the second, rather than of the more Eurocentric term 'Arab Spring' with its connotations of events in Europe in 1989. There is some merit in such an argument, especially as these thinkers dislike the idea that with the carnage in Syria and the ending of democracy in Egypt in July 2013, the spring is morphing into the 'Arab Winter'.

It is important to agree with such writers that the Arab world is most certainly not a homogeneous place. There is vast difference, for example, between Jordan and Egypt or between Tunisia and Iraq. Just because they speak the same official language (classical

Arabic) and follow the same faith (Islam – albeit of two often clashing versions, Sunni and Shia), one cannot say that they are all alike. In Egypt the Muslim Brotherhood sought no allies on assuming power. It aimed to implement its own agenda without collaboration with groups that were more secular. Its expulsion from power in July 2013 is thus not so surprising. But in Tunisia, the Muslim leaders with similar political/religious views were careful to work in coalition. And in 2014, democratic elections were able to take place without conflict. Two Islamic parties, but we see two very different approaches to power in two very distinct countries.

So some parts of the Middle East now have democracy – the protesters achieved their aim. In Egypt one could argue that the nation has gone full circle – military regime, Islamic authoritarian rule (albeit, as one should never forget, actually elected by the people) and then back to a quasi-authoritarian regime again. Syria has descended into barbarity, and with the rise of the extremist movement ISIS (or ISIL) in both Syria and Iraq, an even worse nightmare has come than could ever possibly have been anticipated. In other regimes nothing has changed.

Therefore, as we saw at the start, be careful what you wish for! Protests can escalate into all kinds of events, some for the good and others for the bad. The events of the Middle East in 2011 show this to be true yet once again.

OCCUPY

(2011)

Protests across the timeline of our book have taken all sorts of forms, from great demonstrations, marches, sit-ins to hurling Molotov cocktails from barricades. But one of the most effective is the sit-in, when thousands of protesters arrive at a particular location, settle in and refuse to move. The most famous of these globally were the immensely brave students who occupied Tiananmen Square in Beijing in 1989, with the tragic results that we all know, and similar protests with pro-democracy students in the financial heart of Hong Kong in 2014. On the latter occasion the protesters were removed from their tents but without the carnage of 1989.

Occupy is the name given to the anti-capitalist protests around the world in late 2011, in particular those starting in

New York, in the iconic Wall Street area, in September that year. Then in October 2011 similar demonstrations in London took the same name. These were held in Paternoster Square, near the great St Paul's Cathedral and close to the famous City of London, the hub of global finance in that region.

Zhou Enlai, the distinguished Chinese statesman, is once alleged to have replied to the question 'what do you think of the French Revolution?' with the answer that it was too soon to say. Sadly it is no longer thought likely that such a conversation actually took place. But the principle – that sometimes proximity to events does not give us the necessary perspective with which to judge it – can surely be applied to Occupy since it is very much a work in progress, a non-violent attempt with excellent pedigree, to show the financiers who dominate so much of life what ordinary people really think of them.

Occupy is new but the protests have recent precedents in the demonstrations that have usually taken place with the G8 and now G20 summits. These gatherings of the heads of state of the world's leading nations take place in different countries each year to discuss the economic fate of the world. Sometimes the protests have escalated into violence, but in the past there was no attempt to make the demonstration into a permanent one. In that sense, therefore, while Occupy has models from the past, its decision to have demonstrations all over the world, not in relation to a specific global summit, and to stay put – to *occupy* capitalist ground on behalf of the people – is a new one, and an action that has caught attention everywhere.

It is too soon to say whether or not Occupy will have any lasting impact, other than drawing the attention of a global audience to the recent economic injustices. In particular they have pointed out the iniquities of financial institutions that in 2008 caused such horrific damage to the world's economy and plunged all of us into a recession not seen for well over half a century and more.

In fact, this is what people who have analysed the movement find so interesting and upon which they have pondered. While the Occupy movement are profoundly anti-capitalist, they have come up with one of the best slogans in modern times – *we are the 99%*. Few advertising gurus could have come up with a better and more memorable catchphrase! For surely virtually all of us are in that 99% of ordinary folk whose lives have suffered major disruption by the shenanigans in the financial markets of the 1% who own and run the banks.

But some commentators have asked, what do the Occupy movement wish to *achieve*? In many of the entries in our book the protesters had some very precise and concrete goals – votes for women, a democratic system to choose a government, equal rights for people of African ancestry, the overthrow of a tyrannical regime. All these were achievable goals. But is this what Occupy wants? Or is it a powerful way of making a statement that the 99% cannot be messed around, and that governments of whatever stripe should take into account the 99% of citizens when making policy rather than the financial heft and power for economic blackmail of the 1%? And if that is the case, what precise formulae do they have for helping to bring about these desirable goals? To one acute observer, writing in October 2011 in the New York-based journal *Foreign Affairs*, what Occupy was doing was in effect saying, 'Hey folks – we're here!' Theirs, according to this analysis, was therefore a 'statement protest', gathering together non-violently to remind world leaders of the existence of their democratic base, the 99%.

So this would bring together those wanting the instant overthrow of the entire capitalist system alongside those not normally of revolutionary views but who wanted to make a public and moral statement about the horrors of the kind of greed and thoughtlessness that had plunged the world into recession.

JE SUIS CHARLIE

(2015)

On January 7th 2015 in Paris, two Islamist gunmen, the Kouachi brothers, massacred twelve people at the headquarters office of *Charlie Hebdo*, the French satirical magazine, because they regarded the cartoons published by that magazine of the Prophet Muhammad as being blasphemous. In 2011 the staff had been attacked for similar reasons but had survived, this time, in 2015, they were slaughtered.

In 2006 your author found himself invited to a conversation in London between a former army officer, a Danish diplomat and a leading British Muslim. A Danish magazine had published cartoons of the Prophet Muhammad deemed offensive or blasphemous by many Muslims around the world, and while the Danish cartoonist thankfully survived, the international repercussions were enormous. It was fascinating to watch the dialogue of total mutual incomprehension between the Muslim leader and the Danish representative back in 2006: two people living in the same modern world but inhabiting very divergent mental universes. At least they were speaking to each other!

Today it is possible to see all the controversial Danish cartoons on the web, so because of the ruckus caused at that time considerably more people have seen them worldwide than would have been the case if only the few Danes reading the magazine had read them instead. And it was the same for the cartoons in *Charlie Hebdo* – the pre-massacre circulation was 60,000 in France. But now nigh on *eight million* copies of the special post-slaughter edition have been sold and countless more millions can see them online. Both the Danish and French cartoons are now globally famous.

Many of the entries in this book are past history, whereas the news of the *Charlie Hebdo* killings will have been seen by most readers on television. As of writing, we are still in shock at the tragic deaths of so many people. And in addition, the events are all part of a much wider canvas of Islamic-based terror in Europe, the story of which began in 2001 and which continues. We are part of a tale whose ending we do not yet know, in the same way that people before 1989 could not have foreseen the dramatic and peaceful end of the Cold War in that year.

Millions of French citizens protested at the massacre, and also at the equally brutal murder of Jewish Parisians at the same time. World leaders came to Paris to show their solidarity with France, and countless people across the globe wore 'Je suis Charlie' badges as a token of similar protest against the killings.

France is a country with a strong sense of laicism since the French Revolution in 1789. Overtly religious displays of clothing, including specifically Islamic dress, are discouraged if not in some circumstances actually forbidden. The predominant legal identity of any inhabitant is *French* without the hyphen we associate in other countries – African-American, Afro-Caribbean and similar multi-faceted hyphenated identities. This has been the view in France now for centuries and is ingrained into their culture.

In other nations multiculturalism is more normal, including, for example, the United Kingdom. In the USA religion is deeply respected, but alongside the concept of the *melting pot*, of all kinds of original backgrounds merging together to form a common American identity and citizenship. You can be Italian-American or Jewish-American but either way you are primarily simply an *American*, a US citizen. And it is interesting how well-integrated the Muslim community is in the USA, as opposed to the very different situations that prevail in secular France or multicultural Britain, where integration and radicalisation has proved far more of a problem.

The issue of *Charlie Hebdo* therefore raises all kinds of interesting discussion. Is free speech always *that* absolute? We all protested in favour of free speech after the massacre, but do we believe, for instance, in unfettered freedom of speech for, say, anti-Semites, paedophiles, and, for that matter, Muslim extremists who want to stir up jihad or holy war against the West? If your answer is *no*, then in fact you do not believe in total freedom of expression, and for reasons that are entirely defensible and justifiable. We are, therefore, selective, even though *in principle* we are all in favour of people in a democratic society being able to say whatever it is they believe. There are limits, for the greater good and for the preservation of peace.

Writers in the USA such as the *New York Times* columnist David Brooks, who is on the more conservative side of the cultural debates within the United States, pointed out that the cartoons themselves and the approach of the journalists in France was often simply puerile, and designed to be as offensive as possible. Those taking a different approach argued that however vulgar the cartoonists may have been, and provocative as well, nothing deserves the death penalty meted out to them in such brutal fashion. This applies equally to the other Islamic killers in January 2015 who murdered wholly innocent Jews who had provoked or offended nobody.

So the debate begun by the murders – of Parisian Jews as well as of the *Charlie Hebdo* cartoonists – continues. The killers, as with the similar events in Denmark, ended up giving overwhelmingly more publicity and support for the objectionable cartoons than could ever have been the case had they simply felt their anger privately and left the provocateurs alone. They also gave a major headache to their more moderate fellow religionists, Muslims who want to live at peace in the secular West, however offended they might be by the mores of the twenty-first century.

But we have to ask: is our knee-jerk solidarity with those so violently butchered *always* the right response? How *absolute* is freedom of speech? Is there such a thing as acting responsibly – or were the editors who refused to republish the cartoons acting in a cowardly way in the face of extremist intimidation? The mass protests of outrage and disgust at the carnage in Paris shows clearly where Western opinion lies today. The return of violent anti-Semitism is profoundly disturbing, especially given the memories of 1933–1945, and of similar demonstrations of prejudice in nineteenth-century France and Russia, especially in the pogroms familiar for those who have seen *Fiddler on the Roof*. We live in disquieting times.

CONCLUSION: ONE HUNDRED YEARS OF PROTEST

Protest is not something that comes to an end. As we saw in the introduction to this book, while some events in history, such as wars, arrive at a definite conclusion, protest is an activity that continues permanently, since as one injustice is solved another emerges.

And sometimes the cure is far worse than the original illness, to use a medical metaphor. Look at the French Revolution: were the protesters against Louis XVI really better off under the Terror, the guillotine, Robespierre and then under the despotic rule of an emperor, Napoleon I? Or were Russians happier under Stalin, and the millions he slaughtered, than under the autocracy of the tsars? As several of the entries in this book make clear, we need to be careful for what we wish. All too often the result of protests can have an unhappy ending.

238 | Christopher Catherwood

But there can be a positive outcome as well, or at least an acknowledgement that matters are not as they should be, and that *something* needs to happen. Recent riots in Missouri show that the plight of large swathes of Americans of African descent is not as it should be – racial discrimination unquestionably still exists and has not gone away. But *legally* segregation is outlawed, and in many senses – though clearly not in all – the plight of African-Americans is better than when they were *officially* second-class citizens, right down until the 1960s.

So the citizens of much of the Middle East are tragically worse off as a result of the Arab Spring protests of 2011 – except for fortunate Tunisia, where the movement began and has happily worked out well. By contrast, the inhabitants of the Czech Republic and Slovakia, the successor states to the Czechoslovakia of the Velvet Revolution in 1989, are immeasurably better off. They are now living in genuinely democratic, free and pluralist societies, with the Soviet Union vanished and their old oppressors long expelled. Tahrir Square failed, but Wenceslas Square succeeded – two kinds of mass protest but with radically different outcomes.

And as for the Ukraine, history would seem to suggest that it is too soon to say, since while the Russian puppets have been finally vanquished, the nation stands uncertain, with many enemies holding its eastern borders. With Tiananmen Square in China, it was a tragedy at the time, and democracy is no nearer now than it might fleetingly have seemed possible. Once more, two more squares, two very separate results.

With such results we see that the way in which authorities respond to protests also makes a difference. The Communist authorities in the old East Germany, in Czechoslovakia and in Poland could all have used the 'Tiananmen option' in their respective countries, to massacre the protesters. In Leipzig in 1989 the East German authorities came near to the brink and then backed away. The result was that all three regimes collapsed, a piece of wonderful news for the democracy protesters in places such as Berlin or Prague, but a terrible blow for the Communist cause. And that is a lesson that tyrants have therefore learnt: never give way, or you will go the way of the German Democratic Republic.

So be lucky in your oppressor, like the East Germans, rather than unlucky, such as the Chinese. As we saw, it is often asked what would have happened to Gandhi had the Germans ruled India – he would certainly have been shot. But what if the French had won at Plassey back in the eighteenth century and had conquered India instead of the British, as could have been the case? Would Gandhi or someone like him have been shot? And what would have happened to non-violence then?

Some of the protests in our book have involved the marching of hundreds of thousands of people. In other cases, such as those of the soda fountain in Greensboro in North Carolina, it took the brave stand of just four young men to end decades of discrimination and change the law.

Ordinary people really can make life change for everyone. As consumers we have more power than we imagine. All too often both major corporations and sociologists of the determinist Marxist left join each other in thinking that the masses are powerless, tools for deception and manipulation, helpless against the rampant forces of all-conquering capitalism. But this is not the case, and protests at grassroots level show that if enough of the 'little people' get together they can move mountains. When a British tabloid newspaper trashed the memory of dead football fans, thousands of ordinary inhabitants of Liverpool decided to boycott that paper. People power worked. That tabloid had to apologise, and now there is a legal enquiry showing that those who died were decent, honourable folk who were killed not through drunkenness but through sheer incompetence at the exit gates of the stadium. Protest prevailed and the people of Liverpool won. People who live by corporate power can die by corporate power as well. Democracy is healthier than we think.

In 2014 there were major protests in Hong Kong against the attempts by the authorities in Beijing to limit the democratic choice of the Hong Kong people in the forthcoming elections. Eventually the protesters – who occupied the financial districts of the city in similar ways to the Occupy demonstrators in London and New York – were removed, their demands unmet. But while one could gauge their attempts a failure, it is significant that with so much of the world media present to cover the tent village that the protesters created, no massacre ensued. This was no Tiananmen Square. Was it different because Hong Kong has a special category status in China – democracy may be curtailed, but at least it exists? Or did the Chinese authorities think twice about what would happen if another scene of carnage took place, quarter of a century after the previous events in Beijing? Being ignored was probably a disappointment to the protesters, but perhaps being allowed to live is a sign of welcome change?

Many of the protests at which we have looked are works in progress – we do not know the ultimate outcome. As people legitimately asked the Occupy protesters, what exactly is it that they are trying to achieve? It is hard to say . . .

In conclusion, let us look at two extraordinary women whose protests embody and sum up the story of so many who went before them: Joan Baez and Malala Yousafzai.

Joan Baez was born in 1941. She began singing in the early 1960s, achieving national publicity as early as 1962. She appeared on the cover of *Time* magazine on November 23rd as a folk singer. But it was in the era of anti-Vietnam protest that she became best known.

Here we are looking not at her music per se but the fact that she embodies what has rightly been described as a whole lifetime of involvement with protest movements. One could almost say that if she was not involved it was not worthwhile! While that would be an exaggeration, it is nonetheless fascinating to see the extraordinary degree of overlap between her and so many of the issues raised in this book, which is why she has been singled out here.

Just for starters, she heard Martin Luther King lecture on non-violence and civil rights in 1956. He had a profound effect on her not least because she had suffered racial prejudice. Her father was Mexican and she had his dark skin. She was there in Washington DC in 1963 when Martin Luther King made his iconic 'I have a dream' speech and she was present to sing the civil rights theme song 'We shall overcome'. This became her signature song. Her involvement with that movement was long lasting, as was her strong support of the principle of non-violence, something that as a pacifist she believed in strongly. From an early age she was influenced by the teaching of Gandhi. Her first stance for pacifism came when she refused to participate in a school air-raid drill.

When students began to demonstrate in the late 1960s, she was there again, especially on the campuses in California that were near where she lived. Like many of them she was utterly opposed to the Vietnam War. Indeed, Baez was arrested for protesting against the draft – compulsory military enlistment – and commented that while she had been arrested for attempting to disturb the peace she had in fact been aiming to disturb the war! Significantly, though, she was not a mindless supporter of Ho Chi Minh, the North Vietnamese Communist leader. She was as critical of the considerable human rights abuses of that regime as she was of the USA's support for the corrupt government in the South.

At the same time she was one of the founders of the American branch of Amnesty International, the global human rights organisation that was to honour her later for her decades of support. She is a founder of Humanitas International, and here it is important to note that this group protests at abuses committed by regimes of the left as well as of the right, a politically neutral stand that is sometimes rare. In fact in 1989 she was appalled at the massacre in Tiananmen Square by the Chinese regime and composed a protest song to state this.

The same year saw her in Czechoslovakia, some months before the Velvet Revolution, when such trips were still illegal. She gave her full support to Václav Havel, then a mere dissident, which was repaid with much appreciation after Havel came to power as president of a newly free country. She also visited Bosnia during the civil war there, taking the risk of singing in public in the capital Sarajevo while the conflict was still in progress. And she was against the war in Iraq for the same pacifist reasons that she opposed American involvement in Vietnam. Significantly she spent a year in Baghdad as a child.

She has, like many protesters, been active in environmental politics, and, as up to date as ever, in 2011 became a vocal supporter of Occupy, singing at one of their rallies.

In 2009 a British newspaper recorded her as saying that: 'If people have to put labels on me, I'd prefer the first label to be human being, the second label to be pacifist, and the third to be folk singer.'

Besides these efforts she has been active in campaigns for gay rights, fair treatment of farm workers, Northern Irish peace, nuclear disarmament, Polish Solidarity and peace in the Middle East. One can be sure that if a worthy new cause arises, she will be there too.

Our second example is more recent and much younger, with less experience of life. We have an entry on the heroic work of Martin Luther King, a Nobel Peace Prize-winner (along with Lech Wałęsa of Poland, the Solidarity founder). For decades he was easily the youngest laureate for that award. Then in 2014 it was awarded to Malala Yousafzai, who was just seventeen years old. Will there ever be a younger recipient?

She is now in Britain, but, raised in what had been obscurity in the Swat region of Pakistan, she was an ordinary schoolgirl until the Taliban tried – with near success – to kill her simply for wanting to be an educated girl. When she was only twelve, she blogged for the BBC – not about rock stars or film heroes but about her wishes as a woman to have a proper education.

Her persistent bravery in wanting to be able to attend school was amazing enough as it was, but her campaign on behalf of millions of women around the world since her recovery has been phenomenal. What is taken for granted in many parts of the West is something denied to countless young women like her in far too many countries today.

Her simple protest has now resonated around the world, and she has campaigned, for example, for the hundreds of girls kidnapped by Boko Haram in Nigeria, when politicians from that nation were too cowed to speak. She is just one person, and when she campaigned in the Swat valley she was unknown. Now all of us are aware of who she is and what she has risked for one of the most elementary of human rights: education regardless of gender.

We do not know how her life and her campaign will resonate in future years. But her example shows that a simple protest can, in our modern interconnected society, become global very quickly. She is only one person but she embodies the struggles of many, and she is a heroine for our times. The place for protest and the search for justice never ends.

BIBLIOGRAPHY

Many of the materials used for this book are works of sociology that are alas impenetrable to most readers because of the amount of technical jargon that they employ. So the books below are accessible and non-specialist, but normally cover just the person about whom they are written. However, one book, *The Age of Protest* by Norman Cantor (Hawthorn Books: New York, 1969) is excellent for the protests pre-1970 and is easy to read. Also invaluable are national biographical dictionaries, found in most major libraries and in some cases online. These are the *Dictionary of National Biography* that covers both Britain and India, and the *American National Biography* for the USA. Both are published by Oxford University Press.

 Keesing's Contemporary Archives has been an objective source of reporting on world events since 1931 – more recent volumes have the subtitle of *Record of World Events*. Again it is in most libraries. Wikipedia is also very useful, though as it is self-compiled it is always worth checking against other factual sources to gain a full perspective on the events described.

On individual topics:

Bowen, Jeremy, *The Arab Uprisings* (London: Simon and Schuster, 2013 edition)

Brown, Judith, *Gandhi: Prisoner of Hope* (London and New Haven: Yale University Press, 1991)

Catherwood, Christopher, *A Brief History of the Middle East* (London: Constable and Robinson: 2015 updated and online edition)

Garton Ash, Timothy, *We the People* (London: Granta, 1990)

ACKNOWLEDGEMENTS

In most acknowledgments one reads these days, the author's spouse is thanked at the very end. I believe that that is the wrong place – it should always be at the beginning. So I start with profoundest possible thanks to my wife Dr Paulette Moore Catherwood, who has been my constant inspiration, muse, encourager, best friend and support for nearly a quarter of a century. Without her love and generosity I would never have been able to write anything like as much as I have been privileged to be able to produce. My thanks and gratitude towards her are thus deep and lifelong.

Warmest thanks also to the wonderful folk at Allison & Busby, who have invented the series of books of which this is a part. Special thanks go to Susie Dunlop, the Publishing Director, for having the imagination to commission these books, and to the legendary Richard Reynolds, of Heffers in Cambridge, for introducing me to her. I have also been very fortunate in having Lydia Riddle and then Sophie Robinson as my editor. As can be seen from the dedication page, my father died during the writing of this book, which delayed it for some weeks, and their kindness during that sad period is much appreciated. Many thanks too to copy editors Simon and Fliss Bage.

I am a very happy member of several splendid academic institutions, to each one of which I am most grateful for helping in the research, providing vitally needed facilities, and for enabling me to learn as much as I have about so many different aspects of twentieth-century protest movements. (As always, any faults in this book are my responsibility and not theirs!)

I am writing this in the Roskill Library of the Churchill Archives Centre of Churchill College Cambridge. In addition, it also has the library of the eminent naval historian Captain Stephen Roskill, and it is thus one of the very best places to study the history of the Second World War.

This will be the seventh book that I have had the pleasure of writing here since my ties with the College began, starting with the director Allen Packwood and his team Natalie Adams, Andrew Riley, Katharine Thomson, Sophie Bridges, Louise Watling, Gillian Booker, Amanda Hawkes, Anne Woodman, Sarah Lewery, Jana Kostalikova and Julie Sanderson (all those employed at the time of writing these acknowledgements).

This book is the fifth work I have been able to complete with a grant from the Royal Literary Fund. I am most grateful to Hugh Bicheno, the distinguished military historian, for putting me in touch with them and to Eileen Gunn, their administrator, for making it possible for me to have a three-year living grant to write books.

I have the honour of being linked here in Cambridge to another college, St Edmund's, where membership of the Senior Combination [*sic*] Room is a social delight. I am also grateful to the History Faculty of the University, where I have had the delight of supervising bright undergraduates on the subject of British history since 1867.

I also have the privilege of teaching for the INSTEP Course in Cambridge, which is a programme connected to, among other places, such distinguished American institutions such as Wake Forest, Villanova and Tulane universities along with several equally eminent colleges and universities who also enable their students to spend a semester abroad studying history and other subjects at Cambridge every year. The courses are run by the much-loved worldwide couple Professor Geoffrey Williams and his wife Janice. Over the decades, hundreds of American students have had cause to be grateful to them, along with the faculty that the Williams have put together.

Friends have been of special help in getting this book finished: my wife Paulette and I are profoundly thankful to Andrew and Clare Whittaker, Richard and Sally Reynolds, Lamar and Betsy Weaver, Claude and Leigh Marshall, Larry and Beth Adams, Alasdair and Rachel Paine and Nathan and Debbie Buttery and to their families as well. Lauren Marshall was, as so often, staying with us at a crucial time in the writing process and was as great a support to me and to my wife as ever.

My mother has as always been a profound source of

encouragement in all my writing. As just seen, during the composition of this book she was widowed not long after she and my father celebrated their Diamond Wedding anniversary. So especial thanks to Elizabeth Catherwood for all that she has been, still is, and we all hope will be for many years to come.

CHRISTOPHER CATHERWOOD

CAMBRIDGE, 2015

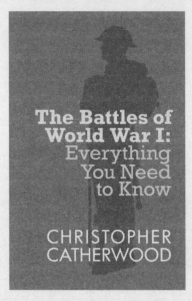

Our understanding of the twentieth century and beyond hinges upon the First World War. In this new and comprehensive book, the fascinating facts are presented in an accessible way, allowing anyone to brush up on the devastating conflict that changed the world we live in.

Discover everything you need to know about:

The battle of Ypres

The Somme

The forgotten wars between Italy, Austria and Russia

The invention of the tank and how it changed the war

The role of the USA

The siege of Kut

The battle the Germans won

and much more . . .

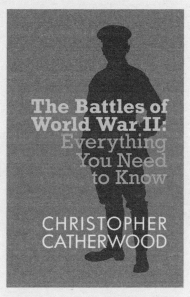

The Battles of
World War II:
Everything
You Need
to Know

CHRISTOPHER
CATHERWOOD

The carnage of the Second World War is without parallel in human history with some estimating a death toll of over 80 million people. This invaluable compendium of interesting facts brings an objective, informative voice to the vast detail of the war's key battles that shaped the society in which we live today.

Discover everything you need to know about:

The Nanjing massacre

The battle for Poland

The battle of Britain

Operation Typhoon and the battle for Moscow

The Dambusters

D-Day

The war against Japan

and much more . . .

To discover more great books and to
place an order visit our website at
allisonandbusby.com

Don't forget to sign up to our free newsletter at
allisonandbusby.com/newsletter
for latest releases, events and exclusive offers

Allison & Busby Books
@AllisonandBusby

You can also call us on
020 7580 1080
for orders, queries
and reading recommendations